Poems children will sit Still for

Poems children will sit Still for *

a selection for the primary grades

Compiled and edited by
the editors of Scholastic's Lucky Book Club
Beatrice Schenk de Regniers,
Eva Moore, Mary Michaels White

SCHOLASTIC BOOK SERVICES
NEW YORK • TORONTO • LONDON • AUCKLAND • SYDNEY

 Published by Scholastic Book Services, a division of Scholastic Magazines, Inc.

For reprint permission grateful acknowledgment is made to:

Association for Childhood Education International and David Ross for "Good Morning" by Muriel Sipe (Mrs. David Ross) from SUNG UNDER THE SILVER UMBRELLA, copyright 1935 by The Macmillan Company.

Atheneum Publishers for "8 A.M. Shadows" from 8 A.M. SHADOWS by Patricia Hubbell, copyright © 1965 by Patricia Hubbell; "Wind Song" and "Dragon Smoke" from I FEEL THE SAME WAY by Lilian Moore, text copyright © 1967 by Lilian Moore; "What in the World?" and "To Meet Mr. Lincoln" from THERE IS NO RHYME FOR SILVER by Eve Merriam, copyright © 1962 by Eve Merriam; "On Our Way," "Big Little Boy," and "Weather" from CATCH A LITTLE RHYME by Eve Merriam, copyright © 1966 by Eve Merriam.

A. S. Barnes & Company, Inc., for "A Funny Man" by Natalie Joan from BARNES BOOK OF NURSERY VERSE.

Rowena Bennett for "The Steam Shovel" and five lines from "The Witch of Willowby Wood" from STORY-TELLER POEMS, copyright 1948 by Rowena Bennett.

William Cole for "Here Comes the Band" by William Cole and for "Oh Did You Hear?" by Shel Silverstein, © 1961 by Shel Silverstein.

Collins-Knowlton-Wing, Inc., for "The Pumpkin" from A GOLDEN LAND by Robert Graves, copyright © 1959 by Robert Graves.

Doubleday & Company, Inc., for "The Bat" from THE COLLECTED POEMS OF THEODORE ROETHKE, copyright 1938 by Theodore Roethke; and "Mice" by Rose Fyleman from FIFTY ONE NEW NURSERY RHYMES, copyright 1932 by Doubleday & Company, Inc.

E. P. Dutton & Company, Inc., for "Day Before Christmas," copyright 1941 by Marchette Chute from RHYMES ABOUT THE COUNTRY by Marchette Chute; "Dogs," copyright 1946 by Marchette Chute, "Our Tree," copyright 1941 by Marchette Chute, and "Weather," copyright 1941 by Marchette Chute, from AROUND AND ABOUT by Marchette Chute, published 1957 by E. P. Dutton & Company, Inc; "Galoshes" from STORIES TO BEGIN ON by Rhoda W. Bacmeister, copyright 1940 by E. P. Dutton & Company, Inc., renewal © 1968 by Rhoda W. Bacmeister; "Politeness" from WHEN WE WERE VERY YOUNG by A. A. Milne, copyright 1924 by E. P. Dutton & Company, Inc. Renewal 1952 by A. A. Milne; "Furry Bear" from NOW WE ARE SIX by A. A. Milne, copyright 1927 by E. P. Dutton & Company, Inc. Renewal © 1955 by A. A. Milne; "The More It Snows" from THE HOUSE AT POOH CORNER by A. A. Milne, copyright 1928 by E. P. Dutton & Company, Inc. Renewal © 1956 by A. A. Milne; "A Pig Tale," "W," and "The Old Wife and the Ghost" from THE BLACKBIRD IN THE LILAC by James Reeves, published 1959 by E. P. Dutton & Company, Inc.

Norma Millay Ellis for "Come along in then, little girl" from "From a Very Little Sphinx" from COLLECTED POEMS OF EDNA ST. VINCENT MILLAY, copyright 1929, 1956 by Edna St. Vincent Millay and Norma Millay Ellis, published by Harper & Row, Publishers.

Follett Publishing Company for "Necks," "Tails," "Gingerbread Man," and "When You Talk to a Monkey" from THE DAY IS DANCING by Rowena Bennett, copyright © 1948, 1968 by Rowena Bennett.

Samuel French, Inc., for "Snail" by John Drinkwater.

Harcourt, Brace & World, Inc., for "Arithmetic" (excerpt), "We Must Be Polite," "Paper I," and "Paper II" from COMPLETE POEMS by Carl Sandburg, copyright 1950 by Carl Sandburg; "Buffalo Dusk" from SMOKE AND STEEL by Carl Sandburg, copyright 1920 by Harcourt, Brace & World, Inc., renewed 1948 by Carl Sandburg; "For a Bird" from THE MOON AND A STAR by Myra Cohn Livingston, © 1965 by Myra Cohn Livingston; "Rain" from WHISPERS AND OTHER POEMS by Myra Cohn Livingston, © 1958 by Myra Cohn Livingston; "who knows if the moon's . . . ," copyright 1925 by e. e. cummings from POEMS 1923-1954 by e. e. cummings; "If We Walked On Our Hands" from SOMETHING SPECIAL by Beatrice Schenk de Regniers, © 1958 by Beatrice Schenk de Regniers.

Harper & Row, Publishers for "First Snow" from A POCKETFUL OF RHYMES by Marie Louise Allen, copyright 1939 by Harper & Brothers; "I Have a Lion" and "If I Were a . . ." (last stanza) from THE ROSE ON MY CAKE by Karla Kuskin, copyright © 1964 by Karla Kuskin; "Knitted Things" from ALEXANDER SOAMES: HIS POEMS by Karla Kuskin, copyright © 1962 by Karla Kuskin.

Florence Parry Heide for "Rocks," © 1969 by Florence Parry Heide.

The Hokuseido Press Co., Ltd., for "Snow" by Issa from HAIKU, Vols. I-IV, edited and translated by R. H. Blyth.

Holt, Rinehart and Winston, Inc., for "Stopping by Woods on a Snowy Evening" from

1st printing .... April 1969

Printed in the U.S.A.

COMPLETE POEMS OF ROBERT FROST, copyright 1916, 1923 by Holt, Rinehart and Winston, Inc., copyright 1944, 1951 by Robert Frost.

Houghton Mifflin Company for "I Met a Crow" from I MET A MAN by John Ciardi, copyright © 1961 by Houghton Mifflin Company.

Tamara Kitt for "So Long As There's Weather" and "There Was a Young Lady from Glitch," © 1969 by Tamara Kitt.

Alfred A. Knopf, Inc., for "April Rain Song," "Poem," and "Winter Moon" from THE DREAM KEEPER by Langston Hughes, copyright 1932 and renewed 1960 by Langston Hughes.

J. B. Lippincott Company for "Mrs. Peck-Pigeon" from POEMS FOR CHILDREN by Eleanor Farjeon, copyright 1933, 1961 by Eleanor Farjeon; "My Cat, Mrs. Lick-a-chin" from YOU READ TO ME, I'LL READ TO YOU by John Ciardi, copyright © 1962 by John Ciardi; "How to Tell the Top of a Hill" from THE REASON FOR THE PELICAN by John Ciardi, copyright © 1959 by John Ciardi; "Lengths of Time" from WONDERFUL TIME by Phyllis McGinley, copyright © 1965, 1966 by Phyllis McGinley; "Little Snail" from POEMS BY A LITTLE GIRL by Hilda Conkling, copyright 1920, 1948 by Hilda Conkling.

Little, Brown and Company for "The Camel," copyright 1933 by Curtis Publishing Company, and "The Duck," copyright 1936 by Curtis Publishing Company, from VERSES FROM 1929 ON by Ogden Nash; "Adventures of Isabel," copyright 1936 by Ogden Nash, from FAMILY REUNION by Ogden Nash; "The Folk Who Live in Backward Town" and "Brother" from HELLO AND GOODBY by Mary Ann Hoberman, copyright © 1959 by Mary Ann and Norman Hoberman; "Eletelephony" from TIRRA LIRRA by Laura E. Richards, copyright 1935 by Laura E. Richards; "I Want You to Meet" (five lines) from TAKE SKY by David McCord, copyright © 1961, 1962 by David McCord; "Jamboree" (ten lines) from ALL DAY LONG by David McCord, copyright © 1965, 1966 by David McCord.

The Macmillan Company for "Rain Poem" from POEMS by Elizabeth Coatsworth, copyright © 1957 by The Macmillan Company; "The Mysterious Cat" from COLLECTED POEMS by Vachel Lindsay, copyright 1914 by The Macmillan Company, renewed 1942 by Elizabeth C. Lindsay; "The Little Turtle" from JOHNNY APPLESEED AND OTHER POEMS by Vachel Lindsay, copyright 1920 by The Macmillan Company, renewed 1948 by Elizabeth C. Lindsay; "To a Squirrel at Kyle-Na-No" from COLLECTED POEMS by William Butler Yeats, copyright 1919 by The Macmillan Company, renewed 1946 by Bertha Georgie Yeats.

Macmillan & Co., Ltd., London, for Canadian rights to "The Prayer of the Little Ducks" from PRAYERS FROM THE ARK by Carmen Bernos de Gasztold, translated by Rumer Godden.

McGraw-Hill Book Company for "Pachycephalosaurus" from A DOZEN DINOSAURS by Richard Armour, copyright © 1967 by Richard Armour & Paul Galdone.

Mary Britton Miller for "Houses" from ALL ABOARD by Mary Britton Miller.

Lilian Moore for "To a Red Kite," © 1969 by Lilian Moore from I THOUGHT I HEARD THE CITY to be published in 1969 by Atheneum Publishers.

Harold Ober Associates, Inc., for Canadian rights to "Mrs. Peck-Pigeon" from POEMS FOR CHILDREN by Eleanor Farjeon, copyright 1933, 1961 by Eleanor Farjeon.

Oxford University Press, Canadian Branch, for Canadian rights to "A Pig Tale," "W," and "The Old Wife and the Ghost" from THE BLACKBIRD IN THE LILAC by James Reeves.

Pantheon Books, a Division of Random House, Inc., for "Snow Melting" from THE CANTILEVER RAINBOW by Ruth Krauss, copyright © 1963, 1964, 1965 by Ruth Krauss.

William R. Scott, Inc., for "My Favorite Word" from OODLES OF NOODLES by Lucia and James L. Hymes, Jr., copyright © 1964 by Lucia and James L. Hymes, Jr.

The Society of Authors as Literary Trustees of Walter de la Mare for "Someone" by Walter de la Mare; and as literary representative of the Estate of the late Rose Fyleman for "What They Said" by Rose Fyleman, and for Canadian rights to "Mice" by Rose Fyleman.

Stanford University Press for "The Firefly" (2nd stanza) by Li Po from A GARDEN OF PEONIES by Henry H. Hart, translator, copyright 1938 by the Board of Trustees of the Leland Stanford Junior University, renewed 1966 by Henry S. Hart.

Nancy Byrd Turner for "A Pop Corn Song" by Nancy Byrd Turner.

University of California Press for "A Mother" by Issa from THE YEAR OF MY LIFE by Noboyuki Yuasa, translator.

The Viking Press, Inc., for "Firefly" from UNDER THE TREE by Elizabeth Maddox Roberts, copyright 1922 by B. W. Huebsch, Inc., 1950 by Ivor S. Roberts; and "The Prayer of the Little Ducks" from PRAYERS FROM THE ARK by Carmen Bernos de Gasztold, translated by Rumer Godden, copyright © 1962 by Rumer Godden.

A. P. Watt & Son for Canadian rights to "The Pumpkin" by Robert Graves and "To a Squirrel at Kyle-Na-No" by William Butler Yeats.

WHEN a favorite aunt is reading to her favorite nephew (and she has her arm around him) she can read Shakespeare's sonnets or Milton's epic verse or T. S. Eliot's *Wasteland* and still hold – if not the child's attention – at least the child himself.

In the classroom, as every teacher knows, it's different. Each of the 106 poems in this book was selected with this difference in mind. They were chosen expressly for a teacher to read aloud to – and with – her class. Every selection invites the listeners' participation – vocal, physical, or emotional.

The poems are grouped into ten categories to make it easier to find poems that are just right to read in sequence. In addition, a subject index invites you to select poems for any purpose of your own.

The selections cover an extensive range of primary-grade children's interests and experiences. There is plenty of nonsense and humor, and there are some sad poems too. (As we all know, reading a sad poem or a sad story can be reassuring to children. It is one way of letting them know that sadness is a natural feeling and a valuable experience.)

For many of the poems, we have offered a few suggestions for reading, or for audience participation, or for possible discussion. But it is well to remember that a poem doesn't *have* to lead to discussion, or art activity, or anything at all. A poem can simply be enjoyed for its own sake. The only rule we would like to insist upon is: *If you don't like a poem, don't read it.* (Enthusiasm and boredom are equally contagious.) We hope this little book will help you transmit to your boys and girls the joy of poetry.

A few hints on reading poetry to children:

If you enjoy a poem yourself, you needn't be a theatrical star to read the poem so that children will enjoy it too. Just remember to:

> Read the poem aloud to yourself before you try it on the class.
>
> Read slowly enough so that children can absorb the images or the ideas.
>
> Read naturally, expressing whatever feelings you really feel. Do not adopt a special hushed poetry-reading voice.
>
> Have a good time. Your children will too.

BEATRICE SCHENK DE REGNIERS

CONTENTS

FUN WITH RHYMES PAGES 13-16

Jamboree, *David McCord* 14
W, *James Reeves* 14
I Want You to Meet, *David McCord* 15
What They Said, German Nursery Rhyme *(Rose Fyleman, tr.)* 15-16

MOSTLY WEATHER PAGES 17-34

Our Tree, *Marchette Chute* 18
Four Seasons, *Unknown* 19
So Long As There's Weather, *Tamara Kitt* 19-20
Rain, Rain, Go Away, *Unknown* 21
April Rain Song, *Langston Hughes* 21
Weather, *Eve Merriam* 22
Rain, *Myra Cohn Livingston* 23
Rain, *Robert Louis Stevenson* 23
Rain Poem, *Elizabeth Coatsworth* 24
Dragon Smoke, *Lilian Moore* 24
First Snow, *Marie Louise Allen* 25
from A Popcorn Song, *Nancy Byrd Turner* 25
The More It Snows, *A. A. Milne* 26
Galoshes, *Rhoda Bacmeister* 27
Furry Bear, *A. A. Milne* 28
I Heard a Bird Sing, *Oliver Herford* 29
Lo, the Winter Is Past, *The Bible* 29
Who Has Seen the Wind?, *Christina G. Rossetti* 30
Windy Nights, *Robert Louis Stevenson* 30
Wind Song, *Lilian Moore* 31
Clouds, *Christina G. Rossetti* 32
The North Wind Doth Blow, *Unknown* 32-33
Weather, *Marchette Chute* 33
To a Red Kite, *Lilian Moore* 34

SPOOKY POEMS PAGES 35-41

from Knitted Things, *Karla Kuskin* 36
Someone, *Walter de la Mare* 36-37
The Pumpkin, *Robert Graves* 37
from The Witch of Willowby Wood, *Rowena Bennett* 37
The Old Wife and the Ghost, *James Reeves* 38-39
The Bat, *Theodore Roethke* 40
Stopping by Woods on a Snowy Evening, *Robert Frost* 41

STORY TIME PAGES 42-45

from Adventures of Isabel, *Ogden Nash* 43-44
The Gingerbread Man, *Rowena Bennett* 44-45

MOSTLY ANIMALS PAGES 46-65

What in the World?, *Eve Merriam* 47-48
The Duck, *Ogden Nash* 48
Good Morning, *Muriel Sipe* 49
The Prayer of the Little Ducks, *Carmen Bernos de Gasztold (Rumer Godden, tr.)* 50
The Caterpillar, *Christina G. Rossetti* 51
Firefly, *Elizabeth Maddox Roberts* 51
To a Squirrel at Kyle-Na-No, *William Butler Yeats* 52
Buffalo Dusk, *Carl Sandburg* 52
For a Bird, *Myra Cohn Livingston* 53
Snail, *John Drinkwater* 54
Little Snail, *Hilda Conkling* 54
The Little Turtle, *Vachel Lindsay* 55
The Camel, *Odgen Nash* 56
Necks, *Rowena Bennett* 56
Tails, *Rowena Bennett* 56
When You Talk to a Monkey, *Rowena Bennett* 57
I Have a Lion, *Karla Kuskin* 57-58

Dogs, *Marchette Chute* 59
The Mysterious Cat, *Vachel Lindsay* 60
My Cat, Mrs. Lick-a-Chin, *John Ciardi* 61
From a Very Little Sphinx,
Edna St. Vincent Millay 62
Who Lived in a Shoe?, *Beatrix Potter* 62
Mice, *Rose Fyleman* 63
Pachycephalosaurus, *Richard Armour* 64
The Steam Shovel, *Rowena Bennett* 65

MOSTLY PEOPLE PAGES 66-79

On Our Way, *Eve Merriam* 67
Big Little Boy, *Eve Merriam* 67-68
Brother, *Mary Ann Hoberman* 69
Paper I, *Carl Sandburg* 70
Paper II, *Carl Sandburg* 70
Day Before Christmas, *Marchette Chute* 71
Lengths of Time, *Phyllis McGinley* 71-72
Here Comes the Band, *William Cole* 72
Politeness, *A. A. Milne* 73
We Must Be Polite, *Carl Sandburg* 73-74
My Favorite Word, *Lucia and James L. Hymes, Jr.* 75
To Meet Mr. Lincoln, *Eve Merriam* 76
Poem, *Langston Hughes* 77
Houses, *Mary Britton Miller* 78-79

SEEING, FEELING, THINKING PAGES 80-85

A Bird, *Emily Dickinson* 81
Mrs. Peck-Pigeon, *Eleanor Farjeon* 81
Winter Moon, *Langston Hughes* 82
8 A.M. Shadows, *Patricia Hubbell* 82
What Is Pink?, *Christina G. Rossetti* 83
The Swing, *Robert Louis Stevenson* 84
How to Tell the Top of a Hill, *John Ciardi* 84
who knows if the moon's, *e.e. cummings* 85

IN A FEW WORDS PAGES 86-89

from Firefly, *Li Po* 87
Snow, *Issa* 87
Snow Melting, *Ruth Krauss* 88
A Mother, *Issa* 88
Conversation, *Buson* 89
Rocks, *Florence Parry Heide* 89

MOSTLY NONSENSE PAGES 90-97

Oh Did You Hear?, *Shelley Silverstein* 91
Nicholas Ned, *Laura E. Richards* 91
from If I Were a . . . , *Karla Kuskin* 91
Eletelephony, *Laura E. Richards* 92
The Folk Who Live in Backward Town, *Mary Ann Hoberman* 93
If We Walked on Our Hands, *Beatrice Schenk de Regniers* 93-94
A Funny Man, *Natalie Joan* 94-95
Old Man and the Cow, *Edward Lear* 96
A Young Lady from Glitch, *Tamara Kitt* 96
A Young Farmer of Leeds, *Unknown* 97
Old Man of Peru, *Unknown* 97
I Met a Crow, *John Ciardi* 97

NUMBERS AND LETTERS PAGES 98-102

from Arithmetic, *Carl Sandburg* 99
Five Little Squirrels, *Unknown* 100
A Pig Tale, *James Reeves* 101
Nonsense Alphabet, *Edward Lear* 102

Biographical Index 103-117
Index of First Lines 118-121
Index of Titles 122-125
Subject Index 126-128

Fun with rhymes

Poems need not rhyme.
And rhymes are not always poetry.
But exploring rhymes is an
excellent language exercise.
Playing with rhymes gives advanced
children (and poets) an opportunity to
make witty discoveries —
and offers the reassurance of the expected
to less experienced children.

When you read "Jamboree," make sure the children let you read it through once without interruption. Then immediately read it again, this time pausing after each question to give listeners time to come up with their own rhymes.

from
JAMBOREE

A rhyme for ham? *Jam.*
A rhyme for mustard? *Custard.*
A rhyme for steak? *Cake.*
A rhyme for rice? *Another slice.*
A rhyme for stew? *You.*
A rhyme for mush? *Hush!*
A rhyme for prunes? *Goons.*
A rhyme for pie? *I.*
A rhyme for iced tea? *Me.*
For the pantry shelf? *Myself.*

DAVID MCCORD

W

The King sent for his wise men all
    To find a rhyme for W;
When they had thought a good long time
But could not think of a single rhyme,
    'I'm sorry,' said he, 'to trouble you.'

JAMES REEVES

Before reading this poem to a group of children, Mr. McCord asked, "Who can give me a rhyme for ladybug? . . . No, not *rug* or *hug*. It has to be three syllables — la-dy-bug."

No one could find a rhyme, of course, and so the poet triumphantly read . . .

I WANT YOU TO MEET

. . . Meet Ladybug,
her little sister Sadiebug,
her mother, Mrs. Gradybug,
her aunt, that nice oldmaidybug,
and Baby — she's a fraidybug.

DAVID MCCORD

WHAT THEY SAID

It's four o'clock,
Said the cock.

It's still dark,
Said the lark.

What's that?
Said the cat.

I want to sleep,
Said the sheep.

A bad habit,
Said the rabbit.

Of course,
Said the horse.

Let's have a spree,
Said the bee.

But where?
Said the hare.

In the barrow,
Said the sparrow.

I'm too big,
Said the pig.

In the house,
Said the mouse.

But the dog said – Bow-wow,
It's too late now.

German nursery rhyme
translated by ROSE FYLEMAN

Mostly weather

Until and unless the entire earth
and sky are imprisoned
in an air-conditioned plastic bubble,
we will respond to seasons and weather.
Because poets and children are
so keenly responsive to the elements,
a great many poems in this
collection record perceptions of
seasons and weather.

Marchette Chute takes an apple tree through the four seasons. After your children listen to her word-pictures, they may want to translate them into a mural to decorate the classroom.

In the city, where the ice cream man may be a more reliable herald of spring than apple trees, children will want to talk about the way a city street looks during the different seasons.

OUR TREE

When spring comes round, our apple tree
  Is very full of flowers,
And when a bird sits on a branch
  The petals fall in showers.

When summer comes, our apple tree
  Is very full of green,
And everywhere you look in it
  There is a leafy screen.

When autumn comes, our apple tree
  Is full of things to eat.
The apples hang from every branch
  To tumble at our feet.

When winter comes, our apple tree
  Is full of snow and ice
And rabbits come to visit it . . .
  We think our tree is nice.

MARCHETTE CHUTE

An anonymous poet sums up the seasons in four lines.

FOUR SEASONS

Spring is showery, flowery, bowery.
Summer: hoppy, croppy, poppy.
Autumn: wheezy, sneezy, freezy.
Winter: slippy, drippy, nippy.

UNKNOWN

Some like rain. Some prefer snowy weather. Some would choose warm summery days. Tamara Kitt doesn't care what happens—so long as it's weather.

SO LONG AS THERE'S WEATHER

Whether it's cold
or
whether it's hot,
I'd rather
have weather
whether or not
    it's just what I'd choose.

Summer
or
Spring
or
Winter
or
Fall—

any
weather
is better
than
no weather
at all.
        I really like weather.

I never feel
whiney
when weather is
rainy.
And when it's
sunshiny
I don't feel
complainy.
        Weather sends me.

So –
Rain?
Let it SPLASH!
Thunder?
CRRRASH!
Hail?
Clitter-clatter!
What does it
matter –
        so long as there's weather!

TAMARA KITT

How do you feel about the rain? How do your listeners feel? It all depends, doesn't it? If there are sunny-day games they want to play, then they may share the views expressed in the nursery rhyme —

RAIN, RAIN, GO AWAY

Rain, rain, go away.
Come again some other day.
Little Johnny wants to play.

UNKNOWN

Langston Hughes tells how he feels about rain.

APRIL RAIN SONG

Let the rain kiss you.
Let the rain beat upon your head with
 silver liquid drops.
Let the rain sing you a lullaby.
The rain makes still pools on the sidewalk.
The rain makes running pools in the gutter.
The rain plays a little sleep-song on our roof at night.
And I love the rain.

LANGSTON HUGHES

The poet does not come right out and tell you how she feels about rain, but good listeners will get the message that Eve Merriam thinks rain is *fun*.

WEATHER

Dot a dot dot   dot a dot dot
Spotting the windowpane.
Spack a spack speck   flick a flack fleck
Freckling the windowpane.

A spatter a scatter   a wet cat a clatter
A splatter a rumble outside.
Umbrella umbrella umbrella umbrella
Bumbershoot barrel of rain.

Slosh a galosh   slosh a galosh
Slither and slather a glide
A puddle a jump a puddle a jump
A puddle a jump puddle splosh
A juddle a pump aluddle a dump a
Puddmuddle jump in and slide!

EVE MERRIAM

Read this poem a second time. Ask your children to listen for the verse that sounds like a light spring shower. Which sounds like a summer cloudburst? Which sounds wintry?

You can enjoy rain whether you are outside in it, or inside watching it. Your boys and girls may want to bring other rain poems to class.

RAIN

Summer rain
  is soft and cool,
  so I go barefoot
  in a pool.

But winter rain
  is cold, and pours,
  so I must watch it
  from indoors.

MYRA COHN LIVINGSTON

RAIN

The rain is raining all around,
  It falls on field and tree,
It rains on the umbrellas here,
  And on the ships at sea.

ROBERT LOUIS STEVENSON

Apparently rain and mice inspire more poets than any other two subjects. Elizabeth Coatsworth is the only poet we know who has combined both in one poem.

RAIN POEM

The rain was like a little mouse,
quiet, small and gray.
It pattered all around the house
and then it went away.

It did not come, I understand,
indoors at all, until
it found an open window and
left tracks across the sill.

ELIZABETH COATSWORTH

Brrr. It's getting colder. If you read this poem to your boys and girls on a day when the temperature is about 40 degrees Fahrenheit or colder, don't be surprised to see the playground full of dragons at recess.

DRAGON SMOKE

Breathe and blow
white clouds
        with every puff.
It's cold today,
        cold enough
to see your breath.
Huff!
    Breathe dragon smoke
        today!

LILIAN MOORE

FIRST SNOW

Snow makes whiteness where it falls.
The bushes look like popcorn-balls.
The places where I always play
Look like somewhere else today.

MARIE LOUISE ALLEN

Did someone say popcorn? When Nancy Byrd Turner wrote this verse many years ago, the way to get popcorn was to pop it yourself. First you shelled the sharp prickly kernels off the cob. Then you put them into a popper — a box made of wire mesh (like a cage) with a long wooden handle. Then you had to shake, shake, shake the popper over a flame.

from
A POPCORN SONG

Sing a song of popcorn
  When the snowstorms rage;
Fifty little brown men
  Put into a cage.
Shake them till they laugh and leap
  Crowding to the top;
Watch them burst their little coats
  Pop!! Pop!! Pop!!

NANCY BYRD TURNER

The class can sing these verses to the tune of "Sing a Song of Sixpence." Ask the children what they think they should do when they sing "Pop!! Pop!! Pop!!"

When you read Pooh-bear's song, your class will be glad to give you an assist (at a signal from you) on the *tiddely-poms*. The children may want to hear the story in which we found this song—or "Outdoor Hum" as Pooh calls it. It is in Chapter I of *The House at Pooh Corner*.

THE MORE IT SNOWS

The more it
SNOWS-tiddely-pom,
The more it
GOES-tiddely-pom
The more it
GOES-tiddely-pom
On
Snowing.

And nobody
KNOWS-tiddely-pom,
How cold my
TOES-tiddely-pom
How cold my
TOES-tiddely-pom
Are
Growing.

A. A. MILNE

The trouble with snow is — it turns into slush. But slush doesn't slow up Susie — so long as she's wearing galoshes. After you read this poem, you may want to write all the slushy-sounding words on the board — *splishes, slooshes,* etc. — then let the children add new ones to the list. Great for phonetics. Great fun too.

GALOSHES

Susie's galoshes
Make splishes and sploshes
And slooshes and sloshes
As Susie steps slowly
Along in the slush.

They stamp and they tramp
On the ice and concrete,
They get stuck in the muck and the mud;
But Susie likes much best to hear

The slippery slush
As it slooshes and sloshes,
And splishes and sploshes,
All around her galoshes!

RHODA BACMEISTER

A reading of Milne's "Furry Bear" doesn't *have* to lead to anything but the joy of listening to it again. It *could* lead to a discussion of other animals that sleep through the winter — or to a library search for favorite bear books.

FURRY BEAR

If I were a bear,
  And a big bear too,
I shouldn't much care
  If it froze or snew;
I shouldn't much mind
  If it snowed or friz —
I'd be all fur-lined
  With a coat like his!

For I'd have fur boots and a brown fur wrap,
And brown fur knickers and a big fur cap.
I'd have a fur muffle-ruff to cover my jaws,
And brown fur mittens on my big brown paws.
With a big brown furry-down up to my head,
I'd sleep all the winter in a big fur bed.

A. A. MILNE

I HEARD A BIRD SING

I heard a bird sing
  In the dark of December
A magical thing
  And sweet to remember.
"We are nearer to Spring
  Than we were in September,"
I heard a bird sing
  In the dark of December.

OLIVER HERFORD

LO, THE WINTER IS PAST

For, lo, the winter is past.
The rain is over and gone.
The flowers appear on the earth.
The time of the singing of birds is come.

THE BIBLE

Of all the elements of weather, wind is perhaps the most mysterious — for who has seen the wind?

WHO HAS SEEN THE WIND?

Who has seen the wind?
  Neither I nor you.
But when the leaves hang trembling,
  The wind is passing through.

Who has seen the wind?
  Neither you nor I.
But when the trees bow down their heads,
  The wind is passing by.

CHRISTINA G. ROSSETTI

At night the wind seems even more mysterious.

WINDY NIGHTS

Whenever the moon and stars are set,
  Whenever the wind is high,
All night long in the dark and wet,
  A man goes riding by.
Late in the night when the fires are out,
Why does he gallop and gallop about?

Whenever the trees are crying aloud,
  And ships are tossed at sea,
By, on the highway, low and loud,
  By at the gallop goes he.
By at the gallop he goes, and then
By he comes back at the gallop again.

ROBERT LOUIS STEVENSON

The specific catalog of wind sounds heightens the feeling of mystery and excitement. Before you read this poem to your class, ask them what sounds *they* hear when the wind blows.

WIND SONG

When the wind blows
the quiet things speak.
Some whisper, some clang,
Some creak.

Grasses swish.
Treetops sigh.
Flags slap
and snap at the sky.
Wires on poles
whistle and hum.
Ashcans roll.
Windows drum.

When the wind goes —
suddenly
then,
the quiet things
are quiet again.

LILIAN MOORE

Tell your boys and girls this is a riddle-poem. Can they guess what the white sheep are? Help them along with a few hints.

CLOUDS

White sheep, white sheep
On a blue hill,
When the wind stops
You all stand still.
When the wind blows
You walk away slow.
White sheep, white sheep,
Where do you go?

CHRISTINA G. ROSSETTI

Some winds are warm and gentle. Some are cool and refreshing. And some winds are *brrrrr!*

THE NORTH WIND DOTH BLOW

The north wind doth blow
And we shall have snow,
And what will poor robin do then, poor thing?
He'll sit in a barn,
And keep himself warm,
And hide his head under his wing, poor thing!

The north wind doth blow
And we shall have snow,
And what will the dormouse do then, poor thing?
    Roll'd up like a ball,
    In his nest snug and small,
He'll sleep till warm weather comes in, poor thing!

The north wind doth blow
And we shall have snow,
And what will the children do then, poor things?
    When lessons are done,
    They must skip, jump, and run,
Until they have made themselves warm, poor things!

UNKNOWN

Did a strong wind ever make you feel like this?

WEATHER

It is a windy day.
The water's white with spray.
And pretty soon, if this keeps up,
The world will blow away.

MARCHETTE CHUTE

TO A RED KITE

Fling
yourself
upon the sky.

Take the string
you need.
Ride high,

high
above the park.
Tug and buck
and lark
with the wind.

Touch a cloud,
red kite.
Follow the wild geese
in their flight.

LILIAN MOORE

Spooky poems

Sometimes it is a spooky subject —
ghosts, witches, screech-owls —
that makes a poem spooky. Sometimes it is
something mysterious . . .
something we don't quite
understand.

Don't worry about what this poem means. Just shiver and enjoy it, and your children will enjoy it too.

from
KNITTED THINGS

There was a witch who knitted things:
Elephants and playground swings.
She knitted rain,
She knitted night,
But nothing really came out right.
The elephants had just one tusk
And night looked more
Like dawn or dusk.

KARLA KUSKIN

SOMEONE

Someone came knocking
  At my wee, small door;
Someone came knocking,
  I'm sure – sure – sure;
I listened, I opened,
  I looked to left and right,
But nought there was a-stirring
  In the still dark night.
Only the busy beetle
  Tap-tapping in the wall,

Only from the forest
   The screech-owl's call,
Only the cricket whistling
   While the dew drops fall,
So I know not who came knocking,
   At all, at all, at all.

WALTER DE LA MARE

THE PUMPKIN

You may not believe it, for hardly could I:
I was cutting a pumpkin to put in a pie,
And on it was written in letters most plain
"You may hack me in slices, but I'll grow again."

I seized it and sliced it and made no mistake
As, with dough rounded over, I put it to bake:
But soon in the garden as I chanced to walk,
Why, there was that pumpkin entire on his stalk!

ROBERT GRAVES

from
THE WITCH OF WILLOWBY WOOD

There once was a witch of Willowby Wood,
and a weird wild witch was she, with hair that was
      snarled
and hands that were gnarled, and a kickety, rickety
knee. She could jump, they say,
to the moon and back, but this I never did see.

ROWENA BENNETT

Some people don't recognize spooks when they meet them!

THE OLD WIFE AND THE GHOST

There was an old wife and she lived all alone
   In a cottage not far from Hitchin:
And one bright night, by the full moon light,
   Comes a ghost right into her kitchen.

About that kitchen neat and clean
   The ghost goes pottering round.
But the poor old wife is deaf as a boot
   And so hears never a sound.

The ghost blows up the kitchen fire,
   As bold as bold can be;
He helps himself from the larder shelf,
   But never a sound hears she.

He blows on his hands to make them warm,
   And whistles aloud "Whee-hee!"
But still as a sack the old soul lies
   And never a sound hears she.

From corner to corner he runs about,
   And into the cupboard he peeps;
He rattles the door and bumps on the floor,
   But still the old wife sleeps.

Jangle and bang go the pots and pans,
As he throws them all around;
And the plates and mugs and dishes and jugs,
He flings them all to the ground.

Madly the ghost tears up and down
And screams like a storm at sea;
And at last the old wife stirs in her bed –
And it's "Drat those mice," says she.

Then the first cock crows and morning shows
And the troublesome ghost's away.
But oh! what a pickle the poor wife sees
When she gets up next day.

"Them's tidy big mice," the old wife thinks,
And off she goes to Hitchin,
And a tidy big cat she fetches back.
To keep the mice from her kitchen.

JAMES REEVES

Why does the very idea of bats seem spooky? Perhaps the last stanza of Roethke's poem answers this question. The poet must have looked closely at a bat. If you and your class have not had this opportunity, you may want to do some library research and at least see some photographs of a bat's face. Even this vicarious experience will make the poem more meaningful.

THE BAT

By day the bat is cousin to the mouse.
He likes the attic of an aging house.

His fingers make a hat about his head.
His pulse beat is so slow we think him dead.

He loops in crazy figures half the night
Among the trees that face the corner light.

But when he brushes up against a screen,
We are afraid of what our eyes have seen:

For something is amiss or out of place
When mice with wings can wear a human face.

THEODORE ROETHKE

This poem may seem out of place in a collection of spooky poems — but if you close your eyes and think of stopping by the dark woods on a dark evening, watching the snow falling, falling . . . well, it feels mysterious and, somehow, *spooky*!

STOPPING BY WOODS ON A SNOWY EVENING

Whose woods these are I think I know.
His house is in the village though;
He will not see me stopping here
To watch his woods fill up with snow.

My little horse must think it queer
To stop without a farmhouse near
Between the woods and frozen lake
The darkest evening of the year.

He gives his harness bells a shake
To ask if there is some mistake.
The only other sound's the sweep
Of easy wind and downy flake.

The woods are lovely, dark and deep.
But I have promises to keep,
And miles to go before I sleep,
And miles to go before I sleep.

ROBERT FROST

Story time

When there is just time for a very short story — and a very funny one — you may want to read these three adventures of Isabel to your class. And because children love to hear a familiar story, they will sit still for Rowena Bennett's short and snappy verse-version of "The Gingerbread Man."

from
ADVENTURES OF ISABEL

Isabel met an enormous bear,
Isabel, Isabel, didn't care;
The bear was hungry, the bear was ravenous,
The bear's big mouth was cruel and cavernous.
The bear said, Isabel, glad to meet you,
How do, Isabel, now I'll eat you!
Isabel, Isabel, didn't worry,
Isabel didn't scream or scurry.
She washed her hands and she straightened her
    hair up,
Then Isabel quietly ate the bear up.

Once in a night as black as pitch
Isabel met a wicked old witch.
The witch's face was cross and wrinkled,
The witch's gums with teeth were sprinkled.
Ho ho, Isabel! the old witch crowed,
I'll turn you into an ugly toad!
Isabel, Isabel, didn't worry,
Isabel didn't scream or scurry.
She showed no rage and she showed no rancor,
But she turned the witch into milk and drank her.

Isabel met a hideous giant,
Isabel continued self-reliant.
The giant was hairy, the giant was horrid,
He had one eye in the middle of his forehead.
Good morning, Isabel, the giant said,
I'll grind your bones to make my bread.
Isabel, Isabel, didn't worry,
Isabel didn't scream or scurry.
She nibbled the zwieback that she always fed off,
And when it was gone, she cut the giant's head off.

OGDEN NASH

THE GINGERBREAD MAN

The gingerbread man gave a gingery shout:
"Quick! Open the oven and let me out!"
He stood up straight in his baking pan.
He jumped to the floor and away he ran.
"Catch me," he called, "if you can, can, can."

The gingerbread man met a cock and a pig
And a dog that was brown and twice as big
As himself. But he called to them all as he ran,
"You can't catch a runaway gingerbread man."

The gingerbread man met a reaper and sower.
The gingerbread man met a thresher and mower;
But no matter how fast they scampered and ran
They couldn't catch up with the gingerbread man.

Then he came to a fox and he turned to face him.
He dared Old Reynard to follow and chase him;
But when he stepped under the fox's nose
Something happened. What do you s'pose?
The fox gave a snap. The fox gave a yawn,
And the gingerbread man was gone, gone, GONE.

ROWENA BENNETT

Mostly Animals

The twenty-seven animals caught in our poetry net range from fleas to dinosaurs. And how did a steam shovel get in here? You'll see.

We would guess that faced with a choice between peanut butter and riddles, 78.9 per cent of children would choose riddles. You will want to allow time after each of these riddle-verses for boys and girls to tell you what animal is described.

WHAT IN THE WORLD?

What in the world
goes whiskery friskery
meowling and prowling
napping and lapping
at silky milk?
Psst,
What is it?

What in the world
goes leaping and beeping
onto a lily pad onto a log
onto a tree stump or down to the bog?
Splash, blurp,
Kerchurp!

What in the world
goes gnawing and pawing
scratching and latching
sniffing and squiffing
nibbling for tidbits of left-over cheese?
Please?

What in the world
jumps with a hop and a bump
and a tail that can thump
has pink pointy ears and a twitchy nose
looking for anything crunchy that grows?
A carroty lettucey cabbagey luncheon
To munch on?

What in the world
climbs chattering pattering swinging from trees
like a flying trapeze
with a tail that can curl
like the rope cowboys twirl?
Wahoo!
Here's a banana for you!

What in the world
goes stalking and balking
running and sunning
thumping and dumping
lugging and hugging
swinging and singing
wriggling and giggling
sliding and hiding
throwing and knowing and
growing and growing
much too big for
last year's clothes?
Who knows?

EVE MERRIAM

THE DUCK

Behold the duck.
It does not cluck.
A cluck it lacks.
It quacks.
It is specially fond
Of a puddle or pond.
When it dines or sups,
It bottoms ups.

OGDEN NASH

Even children with no experience in choral reading can come in strong on the last three words of each stanza. On repeated readings, individual children — as you point them out — can take over on the *Good mornings*.

GOOD MORNING

One day I saw a downy duck,
With feathers on his back;
I said, "Good morning, downy duck,"
And he said, "Quack, quack, quack."

One day I saw a timid mouse,
He was so shy and meek;
I said, "Good morning, timid mouse,"
And he said, "Squeak, squeak, squeak."

One day I saw a curly dog,
I met him with a bow;
I said, "Good morning, curly dog,"
And he said, "Bow-wow-wow."

One day I saw a scarlet bird,
He woke me from my sleep;
I said, "Good morning, scarlet bird,"
And he said, "Cheep, cheep, cheep."

MURIEL SIPE

It takes great empathy and imagination to view the world through any eyes but our own. Whether we happen to be ducks or people, each of us tends to see things from our own point of view.

Before you read this poem, ask your listeners what they think little ducks would pray for. After you read it, the children may wish to make up prayers for other animals. What would a cat pray for? A mouse?

THE PRAYER OF THE LITTLE DUCKS

Dear God,
give us a flood of water.
Let it rain tomorrow and always.
Give us plenty of little slugs
and other luscious things to eat.
Protect all who quack
and everyone who knows how to swim.

Amen

CARMEN BERNOS DE GASZTOLD
translated from the French by RUMER GODDEN

This is a kind of prayer, not *of*, but *for* a caterpillar.

THE CATERPILLAR

Brown and furry
Caterpillar in a hurry;
Take your walk
To the shady leaf or stalk.

May no toad spy you,
May the little birds pass by you;
Spin and die,
To live again a butterfly.

CHRISTINA G. ROSSETTI

FIREFLY

A little light is going by,
Is going up to see the sky,
A little light with wings.

I never could have thought of it,
To have a little bug all lit
And made to go on wings.

ELIZABETH MADDOX ROBERTS

We could not find Kyle-na-no on a map of Ireland, but *Kyle,* in the Irish language, means a narrow inlet of the sea. *Na* means of. *No* means old. So perhaps Yeats' squirrel was in a very small, very old hamlet on a narrow inlet of the Irish sea.

TO A SQUIRREL AT KYLE-NA-NO

Come play with me.
Why should you run
Through the shaking tree
As though I'd a gun
To strike you dead?
When all I would do
Is to scratch your head
And let you go.

WILLIAM BUTLER YEATS

Children will respond to the depth of feeling in this lament whether or not they know about the extinction of the buffalo. But the better prepared they are, whether through a study of conservation or of history, the more meaning this poem will have for them.

BUFFALO DUSK

The buffaloes are gone.
And those who saw the buffaloes are gone.
Those who saw the buffaloes by thousands and
 how they pawed the prairie sod into dust
 with their hoofs, their great heads down
 pawing on in a great pageant of dusk,
Those who saw the buffaloes are gone.
And the buffaloes are gone.

CARL SANDBURG

After you read this poem, give your listeners time to express their own feelings about sadness, and loss, and death.

FOR A BIRD

I found him lying near the tree; I folded up his wings.
Oh, little bird,
You never heard
The song the summer sings.

I wrapped him in a shirt I wore in winter; it was blue.
Oh, little bird,
You never heard
The song I sang to you.

MYRA COHN LIVINGSTON

This little dialog should be read to bring out the dry humor — the first stanza questioning and naive; the second, dry and flat. To what other animals would this same question and answer apply?

SNAIL

Snail upon the wall,
Have you got at all
Anything to tell
About your shell?

Only this, my child —
When the wind is wild,
Or when the sun is hot,
It's all I've got.

JOHN DRINKWATER

One good snail poem deserves another.

LITTLE SNAIL

I saw a little snail
Come down the garden walk.
He wagged his head this way . . . that way . . .
Like a clown in a circus.
He looked from side to side
As though he were from a different country.
I have always said he carries his house on his back . . .
Today in the rain
I saw that it was his umbrella!

HILDA CONKLING

"The Little Turtle" lends itself to a circle game.

First verse: Children hold hands and circle 'round a blindfolded child in the center.

Second verse: On each of the four lines, the blindfolded child points in a different direction; each child pointed out steps into the center of the circle.

Third verse: The children circle in the reverse direction; on last line, the blindfolded child tries to tag one of the four children in the center of the circle. If they manage to escape by slipping out of the circle, he tries to tag one of the circling children. Children may duck to avoid being tagged. They continue circling and repeating the last line until someone is tagged. The tagged child takes his place in the center of the circle — unless it is time to get back to work.

THE LITTLE TURTLE

There was a little turtle.
He lived in a box.
He swam in a puddle.
He climbed on the rocks.

He snapped at a mosquito.
He snapped at a flea.
He snapped at a minnow.
And he snapped at me.

He caught the mosquito.
He caught the flea.
He caught the minnow.
But he didn't catch me.

VACHEL LINDSAY

Who ever heard of a sad poem about a camel — or about a giraffe? Your listeners may have some ideas as to why this is so. Meanwhile, here are some verses for them to enjoy.

THE CAMEL

The camel has a single hump;
The dromedary, two;
Or else the other way around.
I'm never sure. Are you?

OGDEN NASH

NECKS

The swan has a neck that is curly and long.
The camel has one that is shaggy and strong.
But the spotted giraffe
Has a neck and a half.

ROWENA BENNETT

TAILS

The kangaroo has a heavy tail
  She sits on for a chair.
There's scarcely any tail at all
  Upon the polar bear.
But the monkey has the nicest tail
  Of any living thing,
For he can hook it to a branch
  And use it as a swing.

ROWENA BENNETT

WHEN YOU TALK TO A MONKEY

When you talk to a monkey
He seems very wise.
He scratches his head,
And he blinks both his eyes;
But he won't say a word.
He just swings on a rail
And makes a big question mark
Out of his tail.

ROWENA BENNETT

Would you rather have a live animal or a stuffed toy animal? There is something to be said for each. Let your boys and girls say it *after* you have read the entire poem.

I HAVE A LION

I had a cat,
Gray
Soft
Fat
Given to grrrring
Quite softly
And prrrrring.
Slipped off one morning
Near the green glen.
That was my cat
Who was not seen again.

I had a dog,
Noisy and yellow
Very cold nose
Wonderful fellow.
Trotted one evening
Out after a pack
Of dog-footed friends
And never came back.

I had a bird,
Bright blue in a cage
Sang without cause
On his miniature stage.
Sat on my shoulder
Looked in my eye.
Sailed out the window
And into the sky.

I have a lion,
Furry and kind
Sits on a shelf
Near the autos that wind.
Eyes wild and golden
Tail like a tuft
He never will slip out and leave me.
He's stuffed.

KARLA KUSKIN

How many children in your class have a dog? How many *wish* they had one? Well, let them listen to this poem, then draw their dogs — real or wish-dogs. Have an exhibit. It will be fun to see how many different shaped dogs there are.

DOGS

The dogs I know
Have many shapes.
For some are big and tall,

   And some are long,

   And
   some
   are thin,
And some are fat and small.

And some are little bits of fluff
And have no shape at all.

MARCHETTE CHUTE

THE MYSTERIOUS CAT

I saw a proud, mysterious cat
I saw a proud, mysterious cat,
Too proud to catch a mouse or rat –
Mew, mew, mew.

But catnip she would eat, and purr,
But catnip she would eat, and purr.
And goldfish she did much prefer –
Mew, mew, mew.

I saw a cat – 'twas but a dream,
I saw a cat – 'twas but a dream
Who scorned the slave that brought her cream –
Mew, mew, mew.

Unless the slave were dressed in style,
Unless the slave were dressed in style
And knelt before her all the while –
Mew, mew, mew.

Did you ever hear of a thing like that?
Did you ever hear of a thing like that?
Did you ever hear of a thing like that?
Oh, what a proud mysterious cat.
Oh, what a proud mysterious cat.
Oh, what a proud mysterious cat.
Mew . . . Mew . . . Mew.

VACHEL LINDSAY

The next two poems should be read at one sitting. Mr. Ciardi's poem is about a cat who can't make up her mind, and Miss Millay writes about a little girl who has the same problem.

MY CAT, MRS. LICK-A-CHIN

Some of the cats I know about
Spend a little time in and a lot of time out.
Or a lot of time out and a little time in.
But *my* cat, Mrs. Lick-a-chin,
Never knows *where* she wants to be.
If I let her in she looks at me
And begins to sing that she wants to go out.
So I open the door and she looks about
And begins to sing, "Please let me in!"

Poor silly Mrs. Lick-a-chin!

The thing about cats, as you may find,
Is that no one knows what they have in mind.

And I'll tell you something about that:
No one knows it less than my cat.

JOHN CIARDI

FROM A VERY LITTLE SPHINX

Come along in then, little girl!
  Or else stay out!
But in the open door she stands,
And bites her lip and twists her hands,
And stares upon me, trouble-eyed;
"Mother," she says, "I can't decide!
I can't decide!"

EDNA ST. VINCENT MILLAY

Perhaps one of your boys or girls will volunteer to recite the original nursery rhyme that inspired these little verses by Beatrix Potter.

WHO LIVED IN A SHOE?

You know that old woman
  Who lived in a shoe?
She had so many children
  She didn't know what to do?

I think if she lived in
  A little shoe-house
That little old lady was
  Surely a mouse!

BEATRIX POTTER

MICE

I think mice
Are rather nice.

Their tails are long,
Their faces small,
They haven't any
Chins at all.
Their ears are pink,
Their teeth are white,
They run about
The house at night.
They nibble things
They shouldn't touch
And no one seems
To like them much.

But I think mice
Are nice.

ROSE FYLEMAN

Some think mice are rather nice — and some think dinosaurs are nicer! Well, uglier, anyhow.

*PACHYCEPHALOSAURUS (pak-i-sef-a-lo-*saw*-rus)*

Among the later dinosaurs
  Though not the largest, strongest,
PACHYCEPHALOSAURUS had
  The name that was the longest.

Yet he had more than syllables,
  As you may well suppose.
He had great knobs upon his cheeks
  And spikes upon his nose.

Ten inches thick, atop his head,
  A bump of bone projected.
By this his brain, though hardly worth
  Protecting, was protected.

No claw or tooth, no tree that fell
  Upon his head kerwhacky,
Could crack or crease or jar or scar
  That stony part of Paky.

And so he nibbled plants in peace
  And lived untroubled days.
Sometimes, in fact, as Paky proved,
  To be a bonehead pays.

RICHARD ARMOUR

Here is another kind of beast that often prowls city streets and country roads — a kind of mechanized dinosaur.

THE STEAM SHOVEL

The steam digger
Is much bigger
Than the biggest beast I know.
He snorts and roars
Like the dinosaurs
That lived long years ago.

He crouches low
On his tractor paws
And scoops the dirt up
With his jaws;
Then swings his long
Stiff neck around
And spits it out
Upon the ground . . .

Oh, the steam digger
Is much bigger
Than the biggest beast I know.
He snorts and roars
Like the dinosaurs
That lived long years ago.

ROWENA BENNETT

Mostly people

There are preoccupations, thoughts, and images
that relate more to people
than to other animals, and you will find
some of them in this section.

The schoolyard or the gymnasium would be the best place, we think, to try out the various ways of walking described here.

ON OUR WAY

What kind of walk shall we take today?
Leap like a frog? Creep like a snail?
Scamper like a squirrel with a furry tail?

Flutter like a butterfly? Chicken peck?
Stretch like a turtle with a poking-out neck?

Trot like a pony, clip clop clop?
Swing like a monkey in a treetop?

Scuttle like a crab? Kangaroo jump?
Plod like a camel with an up-and-down hump?

We could even try a brand new way –
Walking down the street
On our own two feet.

EVE MERRIAM

How big IS big?

BIG LITTLE BOY

"Me oh my," said the tiny, shiny ant,
"I can crawl all the way up a sand hill,
A hill so high it's as big as a thimble.
Can any creature in the world be bigger than I?"

"Skat," said the green caterpillar,
"I can inch myself all the way across a twig.
Now a twig is really *big*!
Hooray for great, glorious, mammoth, and modest me."

"Gog and magog," said the speckled frog,
"And bilge water. Little ant, crawly caterpillar,
You can only creep.
I can leap!
All the way up to a tremendous lily pad in the pond.
How superiffic can any creature be?
I'll tell you –
He can be me!"

"Oh," laughed the little boy,
"Gangway, skedaddle, vamoose.
Look at me, tiny ant. My finger is bigger than a
thimble.
Look, inchy caterpillar. My foot is bigger than a twig.
Look, speckled frog. My hand can cover a lily pad all
over.
Why, I'm so big I can run in circles, I can run in
squares,

I can reach to tables, I can fill up chairs!
And I'm still growing!
When I grow all the way up, my head will bump the
sky.
I'll have clouds for a bed, and a moon pillow,
And stars instead of freckles on my nose."

(*Is that how big a little boy grows?*)

EVE MERRIAM

This poem is especially for boys and girls who have a little brother at home — or even a little sister.

BROTHER

I had a little brother
And I brought him to my mother
And I said I want another
Little brother for a change.
But she said don't be a bother
So I took him to my father
And I said this little bother
Of a brother's very strange.

But he said one little brother
Is exactly like another
And every little brother
Misbehaves a bit he said.
So I took the little bother
From my mother and my father
And I put the little bother
Of a brother back to bed.

MARY ANN HOBERMAN

Paper people, anyone?

When Carl Sandburg used to read his poetry aloud, he read very slowly, with a Midwestern drawl. You will want to pause long enough after each concept to allow time for the concept to sink in.

PAPER I

Paper is two kinds, to write on, to wrap with.
If you like to write, you write.
If you like to wrap, you wrap.
Some papers like writers, some like wrappers.
Are you a writer or a wrapper?

CARL SANDBURG

PAPER II

I write what I know on one side of the paper
and what I don't know on the other.
Fire likes dry paper and wet paper laughs at
fire.
Empty paper sacks say, "Put something in me,
what are we waiting for?"
Paper sacks packed to the limit say, "We hope
we don't bust."
Paper people like to meet other paper people.

CARL SANDBURG

DAY BEFORE CHRISTMAS

We have been helping with the cake
  And licking out the pan,
And wrapping up our packages
  As neatly as we can.
And we have hung our stockings up
  Beside the open grate.
And now there's nothing more to do
  Except
    to
      wait!

MARCHETTE CHUTE

And speaking of waiting . . .

LENGTHS OF TIME

Time is peculiar
And hardly exact.
Though minutes are minutes,
You'll find for a fact
(As the older you get
And the bigger you grow)
That time can
Hurrylikethis
Or plod,   plod,   slow.

Waiting for your dinner when you're hungry?
Down with the sniffles in your bed?
Notice how an hour crawls along and crawls along
Like a snail with his house upon his head.

But when you are starting
A game in the park,
It's morning,
It's noon,
And it's suddenly dark.
And hours like seconds
Rush blurringly by,
Whoosh!
Like a plane in the sky.

PHYLLIS MCGINLEY

Time can be exciting when it is combined with music to create foot-tapping rhythms.

HERE COMES THE BAND

The band comes booming down the street,
The tuba oomphs, the flutes tweet tweet;
The trombones slide, the trumpets blare,
The baton twirls up in the air.
There's "ooh's!" and "ah's!" and cheers and
clapping –
And I can't stop my feet from tapping.

WILLIAM COLE

POLITENESS

If people ask me,
I always tell them:
"Quite well, thank you, I'm very glad to say."
If people ask me,
I always answer,
"Quite well, thank you, how are you today?"
I always answer,
I always tell them,
If they ask me,
Politely . . . .
BUT SOMETIMES
    I wish
        That they wouldn't.

A. A. MILNE

WE MUST BE POLITE

(Lessons for children on how to behave under peculiar circumstances)

If we meet a gorilla
what shall we do?
Two things we may do
if we so wish to do.

Speak to the gorilla,
very, very respectfully,
"How do you do, sir?"

Or, speak to him with less
distinction of manner,
"Hey, why don't you go back
where you came from?"

If an elephant knocks on your door
and asks for something to eat,
there are two things to say:

Tell him there are nothing but cold
victuals in the house and he will do
better next door.

Or say: We have nothing but six bushels
of potatoes – will that be enough for
your breakfast, sir?

CARL SANDBURG

A suggested language-arts activity: Early in the day, ask your boys and girls to write their favorite word on a slip of paper and hand it in to you. (They needn't sign their names unless they want to.) Then, later, write the words on the blackboard as the basis for a language-arts discussion. And after *that* read them the Hymes' verse about *their* favorite word.

Or simply read this verse as a lead-in for a discussion of favorite words.

MY FAVORITE WORD

There is one word –
My favorite –
The very, very best.
It isn't No or Maybe,
It's Yes, Yes, Yes, *Yes,* YES!

"Yes, yes, you may," and
"Yes, of course," and
"Yes, please help yourself."
And when I want a piece of cake,
"Why, yes. It's on the shelf."

Some candy? "Yes."
A cookie? "Yes."
A movie? "Yes, we'll go."

I love it when they say my word:
Yes, *Yes,* YES! (Not No.)

LUCIA AND JAMES L. HYMES, JR.

Lincoln's birthday might be a good time for reading "To Meet Mr. Lincoln," but you needn't wait till then to introduce this lovely poem to your class.

TO MEET MR. LINCOLN

If I lived at the time
That Mr. Lincoln did,
And I met Mr. Lincoln
With his stovepipe lid

And his coalblack cape
And his thundercloud beard,
And worn and sad-eyed
He appeared:

"Don't worry, Mr. Lincoln,"
I'd reach up and pat his hand,
"We've got a fine President
For this land;

And the Union will be saved,
And the slaves will go free;
And you will live forever
In our nation's memory."

EVE MERRIAM

This is one poem that is more effective read alone rather than as part of a series — and read without comment.

POEM

I loved my friend.
He went away from me.
There's nothing more to say.
The poem ends,
Soft as it began —
I loved my friend.

LANGSTON HUGHES

Wherever there are people there are houses of some kind. Mary Britton Miller presents a capsule review of housing from earliest times to the present.

HOUSES

The homes of our
Earliest ancestors
Were lower than low.
They had no windows,
They had no doors.
If you wished to go in
You went on all fours —
The dirt or the dust
Or the snow was the floor.
It was hundreds and hundreds
Of years before
Men lived in houses
With windows and doors
Or lay down in beds
Or sat up in chairs
Or sat down at table
Or walked upstairs:
Then, as time goes,
It was no time at all
Before houses were built
So exceedingly tall,

They had hundreds of windows
And only one door
And you had to go up
In an elevator.
And now they have grown
So gigantically high
They nudge the new moon
And scrape the blue sky;
And today we live
Like bees in a hive
In the tallest cities
That Mister Man
Has built on this earth
Since the world began.

MARY BRITTON MILLER

Seeing, feeling, thinking

Seeing, feeling, thinking —
isn't that what all poetry
is concerned with? Here we have
singled out a few poems in which
the poets have shown themselves
particularly observant.

A BIRD

A bird came down the walk,
He did not know I saw;
He bit an angleworm in halves
And ate the fellow, raw.

And then he drank a dew
From a convenient grass,
And then hopped sidewise to the wall
To let a beetle pass.

EMILY DICKINSON

MRS. PECK-PIGEON

Mrs. Peck-Pigeon
Is picking for bread,
Bob-bob-bob
Goes her little round head.
Tame as a pussy-cat
In the street,
Step-step-step
Go her little red feet.
With her little red feet
And her little round head,
Mrs. Peck-Pigeon
Goes picking for bread.

ELEANOR FARJEON

Would someone like to come to the board to draw the kind of moon Langston Hughes saw?

WINTER MOON

How thin and sharp is the moon tonight!
How thin and sharp and ghostly white
Is the slim curved crook of the moon tonight!

LANGSTON HUGHES

A poem about shadows can get children talking about other poems about shadows — or even about shadows themselves. Could the same poem have been called "Noon Shadows"?

8 A.M. SHADOWS

Everyone's shadow is taller than really,
The shadows of giants are taller than trees,
The shadows of children are big as their parents,
And shadows of trotting dogs bend at the knees.
Everyone's shadow is taller than really,
Everyone's shadow is thinner than thin,
8 a.m. shadows are long as the dawning,
        Pulling the night away,
        Coaxing the light to say:
        "Welcome, all shadows,
        Day, please begin!"

PATRICIA HUBBELL

WHAT IS PINK?

What is pink? a rose is pink
By a fountain's brink.
What is red? a poppy's red
In its barley bed.
What is blue? the sky is blue
Where the clouds float thro'.
What is white? a swan is white
Sailing in the light.
What is yellow? pears are yellow,
Rich and ripe and mellow.
What is green? the grass is green,
With small flowers between.
What is violet? clouds are violet
In the summer twilight.
What is orange? why, an orange,
Just an orange!

CHRISTINA G. ROSSETTI

THE SWING

How do you like to go up in a swing,
  Up in the air so blue?
Oh, I do think it the pleasantest thing
  Ever a child can do!

Up in the air and over the wall,
  Till I can see so wide,
Rivers and trees and cattle and all
  Over the countryside –

Till I look down on the garden green,
  Down on the roof so brown –
Up in the air I go flying again,
  Up in the air and down!

ROBERT LOUIS STEVENSON

HOW TO TELL THE TOP OF A HILL

The top of a hill
Is not until
The bottom is below.
And you have to stop
When you reach the top
For there's no more UP to go.

To make it plain
Let me explain:
The one *most* reason why
You have to stop
When you reach the top – is:
The next step up is sky.

JOHN CIARDI

WHO KNOWS IF THE MOON'S

who knows if the moon's
a balloon,coming out of a keen city
in the sky—filled with pretty people?
(and if you and i should

get into it,if they
should take me and take you into their balloon,
why then
we'd go up higher with all the pretty people

than houses and steeples and clouds:
go sailing
away and away sailing into a keen
city which nobody's ever visited,where

always
            it's
                  Spring)and everyone's
in love and flowers pick themselves

E. E. CUMMINGS

In a few words

Sometimes a poet can give us a mood
or a picture in just a few words — and the
impact is all the more powerful
because the message is condensed.
In this section are brief poems by
a Japanese poet who lived over 150 years ago,
a Chinese poet who wrote in the eighth century,
an eighteenth-century Japanese painter-poet,
and two very-much-alive-and-writing
American poets.
Children are often inspired by
these small mood and picture poems
to create their own.

Ask your boys and girls if they have ever watched a firefly at night. Then tell them that twelve hundred years ago a Chinese poet watched a firefly at night and wrote this poem about it.

from
FIREFLY

I think
if you flew
up to the sky
beside the moon,
you would
twinkle
like a star.

LI PO

No child is indifferent to snow. If you read this on a snowy day, the children may want to try putting into a few words their own reactions to or observations of snow. Or let them write their poems in reaction to whatever the weather happens to be.

SNOW

I could eat it!
This snow that falls
So softly, so softly.

ISSA

An American poet living today uses seven words to paint a picture — a picture that conveys a profound sense of loneliness. If, now and then, you enjoy introducing an unusual word to your class, you may want to use this poem as an occasion to introduce the word *forlorn*.

SNOW MELTING

snow melting
broken shore
little pine tree

RUTH KRAUSS

Many animal mothers, like human mothers, are especially protective of their babies. In some animal groups it is the male who is the protector. If the discussion happens to lead in that direction, the class may decide to do some research on animal families to find out who protects whom.

A MOTHER

A mother horse
Keeps watch
While her child
Drinks.

ISSA

What is going on here? Your boys and girls will be able to figure it out.

CONVERSATION

An umbrella
And a raincoat
Are walking and talking together.

BUSON

The poem is small, the concept stirring. If they have been studying earth science, your children will be more likely to get the full impact.

ROCKS

Big rocks into pebbles,
pebbles into sand.
I really hold a million million rocks here in my hand.

FLORENCE PARRY HEIDE

Mostly nonsense

If men are distinguished from all other
creatures by the faculty of laughter,
then children (and some gifted adults)
are distinguished by their faculty of responding,
without inhibition, to nonsense.
And if nonsense needs defending, we will call
to the witness stand Josh Billings,
a favorite humorist of Lincoln's day, who says,
"Good nonsense is good sense in disguise."

OH DID YOU HEAR?

Oh did you hear?
The President has measles,
The Principal has just burned down the school,
Your hair is filled with jam
            and purple weasels

April Fool!

SHELLEY SILVERSTEIN

NICHOLAS NED

  Nicholas Ned,
  He lost his head,
And put a turnip on instead;
  But then, ah, me!
  He could not see,
So he thought it was night, and he went to bed.

LAURA E. RICHARDS

from
IF I WERE A . . .

If I were a sandwich,
I'd sit on a plate
And think of my middle
Until someone ate
Me.
End of the sandwich.

KARLA KUSKIN

ELETELEPHONY

Once there was an elephant,
Who tried to use the telephant –
No! No! I mean an elephone
Who tried to use the telephone –
(Dear me! I am not certain quite
That even now I've got it right.)

Howe'er it was, he got his trunk
Entangled in the telephunk;
The more he tried to get it free,
The louder buzzed the telephee –
(I fear I'd better drop the song
Of elephop and telephong!)

LAURA E. RICHARDS

The next two poems, read in succession, should set your children to writing — in verse or prose — their own ideas of topsy-turvydom.

In lines 3, 4 and 5 of the first poem, a very slight pause after *hats, sleep,* and *apple* creates just the right amount of suspense.

THE FOLK WHO LIVE IN BACKWARD TOWN

The folk who live in Backward town
Are inside out and upside down.
They wear their hats inside their heads
And go to sleep beneath their beds.
They only eat the apple peeling
And take their walks across the ceiling.

MARY ANN HOBERMAN

IF WE WALKED ON OUR HANDS

If we walked on our hands
  instead of our feet
And we all ate paper
  instead of meat
What a mixed-up place this world would be.
What a mixed-up
    fixed-up
    topsy-turvy
    sit-u-a-tion.

If we wore our hats
  on our behinds
And all we ate
  were melon rinds

What a mixed-up place this world would be.
What a mixed-up
        fixed-up
        topsy-turvy
        sit-u-a-tion.

If babies worked
    while papas played
If the children gave orders
    and parents obeyed
What a mixed-up place this world would be.
What a mixed-up
        fixed-up
        topsy-turvy
        sit-u-a-tion.

BEATRICE SCHENK DE REGNIERS

Slow reading and a pause after each stanza will give children time to appreciate the absurdity of each situation.

A FUNNY MAN

One day a funny kind of man
Came walking down the street.
He wore a shoe upon his head,
And hats upon his feet.

He raised the shoe and smiled at me,
His manners were polite;
But never had I seen before
Such a funny-sounding sight.

He said, "Allow me to present
Your Highness with a rose."
And taking out a currant bun
He held it to my nose.

I staggered back against the wall,
And then I answered, "Well!
I never saw a rose with such
A funny-looking smell."

He then began to sing a song,
And sat down on the ground;
You never heard in all your life
Such a funny-feeling sound.

"My friend, why do you wear two hats
Upon your feet?" I said.
He turned the other way about,
And hopped home on his head.

NATALIE JOAN

After they have heard the five limericks that follow, advanced primary children should be able to recognize the limerick as a verse form.

Exaggerate the rhythm as you read the verses. Later the class may want to clap hands to mark the main rhythms — three stresses in lines 1, 2, and 5; two in lines 3 and 4.

The first limerick was quoted by President Lincoln when some friends asked him why he did not react angrily to his critics.

OLD MAN AND THE COW

There was an Old Man who said, "How
Shall I flee from this horrible Cow?
  I will sit on this stile,
  And continue to smile,
Which may soften the heart of that Cow."

EDWARD LEAR

A YOUNG LADY FROM GLITCH

There was a young lady from Glitch
Who tried to turn into a witch.
  But she found that the most
  She could be was a ghost,
So she threw herself into a ditch.

TAMARA KITT

A YOUNG FARMER OF LEEDS

There was a young farmer of Leeds
Who swallowed six packets of seeds.
  It soon came to pass
  He was covered with grass,
And he couldn't sit down for the weeds.

UNKNOWN

OLD MAN OF PERU

There was an old man of Peru
Who dreamed he was eating his shoe.
  He woke in the night
  In a terrible fright,
And found it was perfectly true.

UNKNOWN

I MET A CROW

Said a crow in the top of a tree,
"What time is it getting to be?
  If it isn't yet noon
  I got here too soon,
But I'm late if it isn't yet three."

JOHN CIARDI

Numbers and letters

It will be easy for your boys and girls to augment this section on numbers and letters. They can draw on nursery rhymes, counting-out rhymes, and jump-rope rhymes to begin with. Then they can try their hand at making up new rhymes.

The section opens not with a rhyme but with some of Carl Sandburg's poetic and witty definitions of arithmetic.

Someone must have asked the poet, Carl Sandburg, to give a definition of arithmetic. And here are six answers he came up with. Perhaps your class can come up with others.

from
ARITHMETIC

Arithmetic is where numbers fly
  like pigeons in and out of your head.
Arithmetic tells you how many you lose or win
  if you know how many you had
  before you lost or won.
Arithmetic is seven eleven all good children
  go to heaven — or five six bundle of sticks.
Arithmetic is numbers you squeeze from your
  head to your hand to your pencil to your paper
  till you get the right answer . . . .
If you have two animal crackers, one good and one bad,
  and you eat one and a striped zebra
  with streaks all over him eats the other,
  how many animal crackers will you have
  if somebody offers you five six seven and you say
  No no no and you say Nay nay nay
  and you say Nix nix nix?
If you ask your mother for one fried egg
  for breakfast and she gives you
  two fried eggs and you eat
  both of them, who is better in arithmetic,
  you or your mother?

CARL SANDBURG

This anonymous verse offers a little practice with ordinal numbers — along with a lot of fun. What if there were seven squirrels? Nine? Could the children make up rhymes for them?

FIVE LITTLE SQUIRRELS

Five little squirrels
Sat in a tree.
The first one said,
"What do I see?"
The second one said,
"A man with a gun."
The third one said,
"We'd better run."
The fourth one said,
"Let's hide in the shade."
The fifth one said,
"*I'm* not afraid."
Then BANG went the gun,
And how they did run!

UNKNOWN

You might call this a kind of countdown . . .

A PIG TALE

Poor Jane Higgins,
She had five piggins,
And one got drowned in the Irish Sea.
Poor Jane Higgins,
She had four piggins,
And one flew over a sycamore tree.
Poor Jane Higgins,
She had three piggins,
And one was taken away for pork.
Poor Jane Higgins,
She had two piggins,
And one was sent to the Bishop of Cork.
Poor Jane Higgins,
She had one piggin,
And that was struck by a shower of hail,
So poor Jane Higgins,
She had no piggins,
And that's the end of my little pig tale.

JAMES REEVES

Here are the first three letters of Edward Lear's nonsense alphabet. We have reserved the other twenty-three letters for your boys and girls to exercise their rhyming skill. They will have so much fun, they won't even be aware that it is good for them.

NONSENSE ALPHABET

a

A was once an apple pie,
Pidy,
Widy,
Tidy,
Pidy,
Nice insidy,
Apple-pie!

b

B was once a little bear,
Beary,
Wary,
Hairy,
Beary,
Taky cary,
Little bear!

c

C was once a little cake,
Caky,
Baky,
Maky,
Caky,
Taky caky,
Little cake!

EDWARD LEAR

Biographical Index

Dates are given only for authors who are no longer living.

Marie Louise Allen was born in Cleveland, Ohio. She was a nursery school teacher for many years and was inspired by her young pupils to write *A Pocketful of Rhymes.* Since the first publication of her book in 1939, the verses have been reprinted in anthologies, magazines, and textbooks. **(See p. 25.)**

Richard Armour, professor, lecturer, editor, author, was born in San Pedro, California. He contributes light verse and prose to magazines in the United States and England, and he has written nearly forty books for children and adults. His writings are particularly noted for their satire and wit. Mr. Armour lives in Claremont, California, where he is lecturer emeritus at Scripps College. **(See p. 64.)**

Rhoda Bacmeister, educator and writer, was born in Northampton, Massachusetts. A teacher for many years, Mrs. Bacmeister has taught in nursery schools, high schools, and colleges. Her writing includes books on child development for adults, and stories, poems, and songs for children. She lives in New York City. **(See p. 27.)**

Rowena Bennett was born in Merchantville, New Jersey, and later lived in Chicago. She began writing poetry at the age of nine. Her poems have appeared in children's anthologies, magazines, and readers, and she also writes plays, holiday programs, and lyrics. She lives in Galena, Illinois. **(See pp. 37, 44-45, 56, 57, and 65.)**

Buson (1716-1783) was born in the Province of Settsu, Japan, and was fond of painting and reading as a child. He became a master of the *haikai* form of poetry and a distinguished landscape painter. **(See p. 89.)**

Marchette Chute writes for both children and adults and is noted for her historical biographies. She grew up in Hazelwood, Minnesota, where she and her two sisters spent rainy days designing their own paper dolls and writing schoolbooks for them. All three sisters are now professional authors. Miss Chute has illustrated as well as written two volumes of poetry for children: *Rhymes about the Country* and *Rhymes about Ourselves.* **(See pp. 18, 33, 59, and 71.)**

John Ciardi, poet, critic, educator, lecturer, was born in Boston, Massachusetts. He has taught in the English Department of Harvard and at Rutgers University and has been the poetry editor of *Saturday Review* since 1955. He has written many volumes of poetry for adults and children and is well-known for his translations of Dante. He lives in Metuchen, New Jersey. **(See pp. 61, 84, and 97.)**

Elizabeth Coatsworth was born in Buffalo, New York. As a child, she traveled extensively with her family—California, Mexico, Egypt, the Swiss Alps. Later she spent a year touring the Orient. She has written many stories and poems for children of all ages, and was awarded the Newbery Medal in 1931 for her book *The Cat Who Went to Heaven.* She is married to author Henry Beston, has two married daughters, and makes her home at Chimney Farm in Nobleboro, Maine. **(See p. 24.)**

William Cole was born in Staten Island, New York. He has written a half-dozen books for children and many poems, but he is best known for his poetry collections. His interest in collecting began in boyhood when he accumulated files of things for no particular reason except that they appealed to him. He is married, has two daughters, and lives in New York City. **(See p. 72.)**

Hilda Conkling, daughter of a poet, Grace Hazard Conkling, was born in Catskill-on-Hudson, New York. A celebrated child prodigy, Hilda Conkling began to make up poems at the age of four and had her first volume, *Poems by a Little Girl,* published when she was nine. A second volume, *Shoes of the Wind* was published two years later. **(See p. 54.)**

Edward Estlin Cummings (1894-1962) was most famous for his poems and the unconventional typographical style in which they were printed. He was born in Cambridge, Massachusetts, and lived in Paris and New York City. In addition to many volumes of poetry, he wrote several plays, a novel, and a book for children (*Fairy Tales*). He also won recognition as a painter. **(See p. 85.)**

Carmen Bernos de Gasztold was born in Arcachon, France. She wrote a series of poems, *Prayers from the Ark,* at the time of the German occupation during World War II. The poems were translated by Rumer Godden, and one of them, "The Prayer of the Little Ducks," appears in this collection. After the War Miss de Gasztold became ill and was nursed back to health by nuns at the Benedictine Abbey at Limon-par-Igny. She continues to live at the Abbey and has written other poems and books for children. *Creatures' Choir* has also been translated by Rumer Godden. **(See p. 50.)**

Walter de la Mare (1873-1956) was born in Kent, England. He began writing in high school where he founded a school paper. When he was seventeen years old he left school and for the next eighteen years he worked in the statistical department of an oil company. During that time he continued to write, and at the age of thirty-five he received a pension which allowed him to spend all of his time writing. He is noted for his fanciful and beautiful stories, poems, nursery rhymes, and nonsense lyrics. **(See pp. 36-37.)**

Beatrice Schenk de Regniers grew up in Crawfordsville, Indiana. Before she wrote for children she danced for them as a member of a theater-dance group in Chicago. Mrs. de Regniers has written more than twenty books for children, a number of which have won awards (*A Little House of Your Own*, *The Snow Party*, *The Shadow Book*, *May I Bring a Friend?*). She has been editor of *Scholastic*'s Lucky Book Club since its inception in 1961. **(See pp. 93-94.)**

Emily Dickinson (1830-1886) was born and grew up in Amherst, Massachusetts, and died there. Only about a half-dozen of her poems were published during her lifetime – all anonymously. Her fame as a poet came posthumously when hundreds of her poems were discovered neatly stacked in a bureau drawer. **(See p. 81.)**

John Drinkwater (1882-1937), poet, playwright, biographer, was born in London, England. At fifteen he went to work in an insurance office and remained in that business for twelve years. During that time, however, the theater was his real interest. By 1912 he was engaged in a full-time literary career, and in 1918 he attained fame with his play *Abraham Lincoln*. Among his many works are two volumes of poetry for children, *All About Me* and *More About Me*. **(See p. 54.)**

Eleanor Farjeon (1881-1965) was born in London into a lively and Bohemian literary household. Of her novelist father she once said he "had a way of turning such occasions as Christmas, birthdays, holidays, and parties into fairy tales." Miss Farjeon typed her poems and stories at seven, wrote opera librettos at sixteen, and published adult and children's fiction, music, games, and plays. **(See p. 81.)**

Robert Frost (1875-1963) was born in San Francisco, California, but moved to New England when he was ten years old. He began to write poetry as a young man and continued to write for some twenty years without success in finding a publisher. In 1912 he moved to England and within a few months his first two books were published. With the second book, *North of Boston*, he won recognition in England, and upon his return to the states in 1915, found himself famous. He wrote more than a dozen volumes of poetry, and was awarded the Pulitzer prize four times. **(See p. 41.)**

Rose Fyleman (1877-1957) was born in Nottingham, England. When she was a little girl, she wrote stories and verses, and one of her poems was printed in a local newspaper when she was about ten. She taught school for a short time and studied singing before devoting all of her time to writing for children. She is best known for her poems, mostly about fairies and elves. **(See pp. 15-16 and 63.)**

Rumer Godden was born in England, but spent her early childhood in India. She writes for both children and adults and has done the beautiful English translation of Carmen de Gasztold's book *Prayers from the Ark.* **(See p. 50.)**

Robert Graves was born in London, England, one of ten children of the Irish poet, Alfred Percival Graves. In his youth he had an opportunity to read more books than most children do, as the library in the Graves' home held four or five thousand volumes. Mr. Graves has written numerous poems, novels, essays, and historical pieces. He has eight children and has lived in Marjorca, Spain, for many years. **(See p. 37.)**

Florence Parry Heide did not begin writing until most of her five children were grown up. Since then she has published almost a dozen picture-story books for boys and girls, several of them in collaboration with Sylvia Worth Van Clief. Some of the best-known books are *That's What Friends Are For*, *Some Things Are Scary*, and *Benjamin Budge and Barnaby Ball.* Mrs. Heide was born in Pittsburgh, Pennsylvania, and lives in Kenosha, Wisconsin. **(See p. 89.)**

Oliver Herford (1863-1935), Anglo-American poet, illustrator, and humorist, was born in Sheffield, England, but moved to the United States when he was six. For many years he contributed verses and drawings to *Harper's Weekly* and other magazines. He also wrote and illustrated about fifty books of nonsense. Mr. Herford and his wife lived in Gramercy Park in New York City for more than thirty years. **(See p. 29.)**

Mary Ann Hoberman was born in Stamford, Connecticut. She has published a half-dozen books for boys and girls, some of them illustrated by her husband, Norman

Hoberman. The Hobermans have three children and live in New York City. **(See pp. 69 and 93.)**

Patricia Hubbell was born in Bridgeport, Connecticut. She has written two books of verse for children, *The Apple Vendor's Fair* and *8 A.M. Shadows*. A lifelong horsewoman, Miss Hubbell also writes a weekly column, "Kennel and Stable" for the *Bridgeport Sunday Post*. She and her husband, a newspaperman, and their two children live in Easton, Connecticut. **(See p. 82.)**

Langston Hughes (1902-1967), author, playwright, poet, song lyricist, and lecturer, was born in Joplin, Missouri. His maternal grandparents were free Negroes before Emancipation and were active in the Underground Railroad. As a very young man, Hughes spent three years working his way around Africa and Europe. His first books were published in the late twenties when he was a student at Lincoln University. His poetry has been translated into six languages and set to music. In addition to books for adults, Langston Hughes wrote several non-fiction books for children. **(See pp. 21, 77, and 82.)**

Lucia and James L. Hymes, Jr., met when they were graduate students at Teachers College, Columbia University. Dr. Hymes, a nationally known specialist in child development and education, has written many books for parents and teachers. He was born in New York City. Lucia Hymes grew up in Marietta, Ohio, and studied education and art in New York. She has collaborated with her husband to write two books of verse for children, *Hooray for Chocolate* and *Oodles of Noodles*. The Hymes have three children and live in Washington, D.C. **(See p. 75.)**

Issa (1763-1828), Japanese poet, was born in the Province of Shinano, Japan. His childhood, dominated by a cruel stepmother, was often sad and lonely. At the age of six he made up his widely known *haiku* verse "No mother! No father!/Little orphan sparrow,/Come play with me." Issa composed some fifteen thousand poems. **(See pp. 87 and 88.)**

Natalie Joan—Could Natalie Joan be a pen name? Except for two other poems signed Natalie Joan which appear in an out-of-print anthology, no record of this author can be found. **(See pp. 94-95.)**

Tamara Kitt was born at sea on the *S.S. Lafayette.* She was educated privately as she never lived in one place long enough to attend school. Her primary interest is folklore, and many of her books for children are based on folklore motifs. Miss Kitt wrote a poem and a limerick especially for this collection. **(See pp. 19-20 and 96.)**

Ruth Krauss has published more than twenty-five books—most of them picture-story books for young children. She has studied music, art, and anthropology, illustrated two of her books, likes to put on plays and write them, and collects children's dreams, poems, and humor. She lives on the waterfront in Rowayton, Connecticut, with her husband, children's author and illustrator, Crockett Johnson. **(See p. 88.)**

Karla Kuskin, children's author and illustrator, was born in New York City. Her first book to be published, *Roar and More,* was originally a part of her thesis at Yale University. Since then she has published more than a dozen books of prose and poetry. Mrs. Kuskin is married to an oboist, has a son and a daughter, and lives in

New York City in Brooklyn Heights. **(See pp. 36, 57-58, and 91.)**

Edward Lear (1812-1888) thought of himself primarily as a landscape painter (Queen Victoria was once his pupil), but he is best remembered for his limericks and other nonsense verse. He was born in London, England, the youngest son in a family of twelve children. He began selling drawings of birds as a young boy, and when he was twenty years old the Earl of Derby invited him to live and sketch on his estate. It was there, to entertain the children, that Lear began composing nonsense verse. When he was thirty-four years old, the verses were collected and *A Book of Nonsense* was published. He also wrote four other books of nonsense and several books on natural history and travel. **(See pp. 96 and 102.)**

Vachel Lindsay (1879-1931) was born in Springfield, Illinois. As a young man he wandered throughout the United States, reciting his poems in return for food and lodging and distributing a leaflet called *Rhymes to Be Traded for Bread*. He used strong, insistent rhythms in his poetry, and its effect is best felt when the poems are read, chanted, or sung aloud. **(See pp. 55 and 60.)**

Li Po (about 700-762), Chinese poet, was born in Szechwan Province, China. He liked to roam, loaf, mountain-climb, and drink. Tradition has it that he died by drowning in an effort to embrace the image of the moon in a river. Li Po is considered to be one of the two greatest Chinese poets of his period. **(See p. 87.)**

Myra Cohn Livingston looks upon her poetry for children as a reflection of her own happy childhood. Growing up in Omaha, Nebraska, she had dozens of friends and cousins to play with. She wrote poetry at five, plays that were produced in school, and showed talent for both music and sculpture. Mrs. Livingston lives in Los Angeles, California, with her husband and three children. **(See pp. 23 and 53.)**

David McCord was born in New York City but spent his boyhood in Oregon, part of it on a ranch. He began to write verse when he was fifteen, and he contributed verse and prose to a daily paper in Portland, Oregon, and to his high school magazine. He is known primarily for his poetry, but also writes prose, essays, and articles, and has had several one-man exhibits of his water colors. **(See pp. 14 and 15.)**

Phyllis McGinley was born in Ontario, Oregon, and spent her early childhood on a ranch in eastern Colorado. She began to write verse at the age of six. She has received many awards for her light verse, and in 1961 she was recipient of the Pulitzer prize for poetry. She was married to Charles Hayden in 1937, and has lived ever since in Larchmont, New York. **(See pp. 71-72.)**

Eve Merriam is a free-lance writer, poet, and lecturer, and has received many awards for her adult poetry. Several of her books are for children. Miss Merriam was born in Philadelphia, Pennsylvania. She says, "I always wrote – even when I was young." She has also conducted a radio program and worked as a magazine and book editor. She and her husband, also a writer, and her two teen-age sons live in New York City. **(See pp. 22, 47-48, 67, 67-68, and 76.)**

Edna St. Vincent Millay (1892-1950) was born in Rockland, Maine, and began writing verse as a young girl.

She was graduated from Vassar College in 1917 and moved to New York City where she lived in Greenwich Village among other noted writers of the twenties and thirties. Miss Millay became interested in the theater and wrote several plays in verse and an opera libretto. In 1923 she was awarded the Pulitzer prize for her book, *The Harp Weaver and Other Poems.* Although she did not write expressly for children, many of her poems are suitable for them. **(See p. 62.)**

Mary Britton Miller, author and poet, was born in New London, Connecticut. She writes novels and poetry, and contributes short stories to magazines. Her books for children include *Jungle Journey* and *Listen – the Birds.* Miss Miller lives in New York City. **(See pp. 78-79.)**

A. A. Milne (1882-1956) was born and lived in London, England. He began writing verses and parodies in prep school. Later, his three-year-old son, Christopher Robin, and memories of his own boyhood inspired him to write verse for young people. Two volumes of verse and two story books were created about the characters of Christopher Robin and Winnie-the-Pooh and other nursery animals. Besides his books for children, Mr. Milne wrote several adult plays and a detective story. **(See pp. 26, 28, and 73.)**

Lilian Moore, editor and author, was born and lives in New York City. She has been a teacher and reading specialist with the New York City Board of Education, and is a special-projects editor and consultant for various publishers. She writes stories and poetry for children and has published more than fifteen books. **(See pp. 24, 31, and 34.)**

Ogden Nash was born in Rye, New York. He studied at Harvard and worked in a publishing house for a number of years before becoming a full-time writer. Mr. Nash has had published many stories and books of humorous verse – several of them for children. In 1943 he collaborated with the late Kurt Weill to write the musical comedy *One Touch of Venus*. Mr. Nash lives in Baltimore, Maryland. **(See pp. 43-44, 48, and 56.)**

Beatrix Potter (1866-1943) grew up in London in a stuffy, Victorian household. She was shy with adults but had a warm, open relationship with children. *The Tale of Peter Rabbit* was first written in letter form to a five-year-old friend. Beatrix Potter did most of her writing in the ten years that followed the publication of *Peter Rabbit*. At the age of forty-seven, she married a country lawyer and settled into the country life she loved. She became an expert on sheep breeding and was active in land conservation projects. **(See p. 62.)**

James Reeves, poet, critic, anthologist, teacher, was born in Harrow, Middlesex, England. He is noted for his poetry collections (his own and others) and for his retellings of English fairy tales, Bible stories, and legends. Mr. Reeves lives in Sussex, England. **(See pp. 14, 38-39, and 101.)**

Laura E. Richards (1850-1943) was born in Boston, Massachusetts, one of six children of Doctor Samuel G. Howe, renowned for his work with the blind, and Julia Ward Howe, author of "The Battle Hymn of the Republic." Mrs. Howe sang to her children often, and Laura memorized songs and ballads before she could read. Years later, she made up jingles to sing to her own children. Some of them were published, and her writing career began. She wrote nearly seventy-five books of poetry and prose for boys and girls and several biographies for adults. **(See pp. 91 and 92.)**

Elizabeth Maddox Roberts (1886-1941) was born in Springfield, Kentucky. She was educated at the University of Chicago where she wrote prize-winning essays and poems. After graduation she moved to New York to follow a writing career. She wrote short stories, poetry, and several adult novels – the most famous among them, *The Time of Man.* Her volume of verse, *Under the Tree,* has become a classic in children's literature. **(See p. 51.)**

Theodore Roethke (1908-1963) was born in Saginaw, Michigan, and grew up in and around a beautiful, family-owned greenhouse. He took intense pleasure in nursery rhymes as a child, and had dreams of a literary career while still a young boy. He began to write poetry at Harvard. In 1954 he was awarded the Pulitzer prize for his volume of poems *The Waking.* He taught at various colleges and was a professor of English at the University of Washington in Seattle at the time of his death. **(See p. 40.)**

Christina G. Rossetti (1830-1894) lived all her life in London. She was from a poor but intellectual family and was educated by her mother, for whom she wrote her first poem at the age of eleven. She gained recognition as a poet in her early thirties after the publication of *Goblin Market*, a story in verse. She was a frail, serious-minded, and religious woman who spent the last eighteen years of her life in semi-seclusion. **(See pp. 30, 32, 51, and 83.)**

Carl Sandburg (1878-1967), poet, biographer, collector and singer of folksongs, was born in Galesburg, Illinois.

He worked as a newspaperman in Chicago for many years, wrote poetry, and frequently toured the United States with his guitar, singing folksongs and reciting his poems. He spent thirty years preparing a monumental six-volume biography of Lincoln, and in 1940 was awarded the Pulitzer prize in history for the last four volumes, *Abraham Lincoln: the War Years.* In 1950 he received the Pulitzer prize in poetry for his work, *Complete Poems.* For children he wrote: *Abe Lincoln Grows Up, Early Moon, Rootabaga Stories, Potato Face.* **(See pp. 52, 70, 73-74, and 99.)**

Shelley Silverstein was born in Chicago, Illinois. He is a poet, song-writer, performer (he has recorded several of his songs), writer of children's books, and roving cartoonist for *Playboy* magazine. **(See p. 91.)**

Muriel Sipe – In spite of diligent research, we were unable to turn up biographical material on Muriel Sipe. We found only that her married name is (was) Mrs. David Ross and that her poem "Good Morning" has been reprinted in many children's anthologies. It may be that "Good Morning" is her only published work. If any of our readers have information about Muriel Sipe, let us know. We will include it in a future edition of this anthology. **(See p. 49.)**

Robert Louis Stevenson (1850-1894) was born in Edinburgh, Scotland, the son of a lighthouse builder. He was a semi-invalid from birth and spent much of his childhood in bed where he made up verses and stories long before he could write. To please his father he studied engineering and law, but never practiced either profession. Instead, he wandered throughout France, Germany, and Scotland and wrote about his travels. He married when he was thirty, and it was during the remaining fourteen years of his life that he wrote his famous tales and poems. **(See pp. 23, 30, and 84.)**

Nancy Byrd Turner was born in Boydton, Virginia. She has been an editor as well as a writer and has published poetry, a biography, and several books for children. Her poems have appeared in magazines and anthologies and have been set to music by Hoagy Carmichael and other composers. **(See p. 25.)**

William Butler Yeats (1865-1939) was born in Dublin, Ireland, the son of a well-known painter. Because his father wished it, Yeats studied painting for a while, but soon discovered that he was a poet, not a painter. In addition to poetry, he wrote plays in prose and verse, and essays. In 1923 he was awarded the Nobel prize for literature. **(See p. 52.)**

Index of First Lines

A bird came down the walk **81**
A little light is going by **51**
A mother horse **88**
A rhyme for ham? Jam **14**
A was once an apple pie **102**
Among the later dinosaurs **64**
An umbrella **89**
Arithmetic is where numbers fly **99**

Behold the duck **48**
Big rocks into pebbles **89**
Breathe and blow **24**
Brown and furry **51**
By day the bat is cousin to the mouse **40**

Come along in then, little girl! **62**
Come play with me **52**

Dear God **50**
Dot a dot dot dot a dot dot **22**

Everyone's shadow is taller than really **82**

Five little squirrels **100**
Fling **34**
For, lo, the winter is past **29**

How do you like to go up in a swing **84**
How thin and sharp is the moon tonight! **82**

I could eat it! **87**
I found him lying near the tree; I folded up his wings **53**
I had a cat **57**
I had a little brother **69**
I heard a bird sing **29**
I loved my friend **77**
I saw a little snail **54**
I saw a proud, mysterious cat **60**
I think **87**
I think mice **63**
I write what I know on one side of the paper **70**
If I lived at the time **76**
If I were a bear **28**
If I were a sandwich **91**
If people ask me **73**
If we meet a gorilla **73**
If we walked on our hands **93**
Isabel met an enormous bear **43**
It is a windy day **33**
It's four o'clock **15**

Let the rain kiss you **21**

. . . Meet Ladybug **15**
"Me oh my," said the tiny, shiny ant **67**
Mrs. Peck-Pigeon **81**

Nicholas Ned **91**

Oh did you hear? **91**
Once there was an elephant **92**
One day a funny kind of man **94**
One day I saw a downy duck **49**

Paper is two kinds, to write on, to wrap with **70**
Poor Jane Higgins **101**

Rain, rain, go away **21**

Said a crow in the top of a tree **97**
Sing a song of popcorn **25**
Snail upon the wall **54**
Snow makes whiteness where it falls **25**
snow melting **88**
Some of the cats I know about **61**
Someone came knocking **36**
Spring is showery, flowery, bowery **19**
Summer rain **23**
Susie's galoshes **27**

The band comes booming down the street **72**
The buffaloes are gone **52**
The camel has a single hump **56**
The dogs I know **59**
The folk who live in Backward town **93**
The gingerbread man gave a gingery shout **44**
The homes of our **78**
The kangaroo has a heavy tail **56**
The King sent for his wise men all **14**
The more it **26**
The north wind doth blow **32**
The rain is raining all around **23**
The rain was like a little mouse **24**
The steam digger **65**
The swan has a neck that is curly and long **56**
The top of a hill **84**
There is one word **75**
There once was a witch of Willowby Wood **37**
There was a little turtle **55**
There was a witch who knitted things **36**
There was a young farmer of Leeds **97**
There was a young lady from Glitch **96**
There was an old man of Peru **97**
There was an Old Man who said, "How **96**
There was an old wife and she lived all alone **38**
Time is peculiar **71**

We have been helping with the cake **71**
What in the world **47**
What is pink? a rose is pink **83**
What kind of walk shall we take today? **67**
When spring comes round, our apple tree **18**
When the wind blows **31**
When you talk to a monkey **57**
Whenever the moon and stars are set **30**
Whether it's cold **19**
White sheep, white sheep **32**
Who has seen the wind? **30**
who knows if the moon's **85**
Whose woods these are I think I know **41**

You know that old woman **62**
You may not believe it, for hardly could I **37**

Index of Titles

from Adventures of Isabel, *Ogden Nash* **43-44**
April Rain Song, *Langston Hughes* **21**
from Arithmetic, *Carl Sandburg* **99**

Bat, The, *Theodore Roethke* **40**
Big Little Boy, *Eve Merriam* **67-68**
Bird, A, *Emily Dickinson* **81**
Brother, *Mary Ann Hoberman* **69**
Buffalo Dusk, *Carl Sandburg* **52**

Camel, The, *Ogden Nash* **56**
Caterpillar, The, *Christina G. Rossetti* **51**
Clouds, *Christina G. Rossetti* **32**
Conversation, *Buson* **89**

Day Before Christmas, *Marchette Chute* **71**
Dogs, *Marchette Chute* **59**
Dragon Smoke, *Lilian Moore* **24**
Duck, The, *Ogden Nash* **48**

8 A.M. Shadows, *Patricia Hubbell* **82**
Eletelephony, *Laura E. Richards* **92**

Firefly, *Elizabeth Maddox Roberts* **51**
from Firefly, *Li Po* **87**
First Snow, *Marie Louise Allen* **25**
Five Little Squirrels, *Unknown* **100**
Folk Who Live in Backward Town, The,
Mary Ann Hoberman **93**
For a Bird, *Myra Cohn Livingston* **53**

Four Seasons, *Unknown* **19**
From a Very Little Sphinx, *Edna St. Vincent Millay* **62**
Funny Man, A, *Natalie Joan* **94-95**
Furry Bear, *A. A. Milne* **28**

Galoshes, *Rhoda Bacmeister* **27**
Gingerbread Man, The, *Rowena Bennett* **44-45**
Good Morning, *Muriel Sipe* **49**

Here Comes the Band, *William Cole* **72**
Houses, *Mary Britton Miller* **78-79**
How to Tell the Top of a Hill, *John Ciardi* **84**

I Have a Lion, *Karla Kuskin* **57-58**
I Heard a Bird Sing, *Oliver Herford* **29**
I Met a Crow, *John Ciardi* **97**
I Want You to Meet, *David McCord* **15**
from If I Were a . . . , *Karla Kuskin* **91**
If We Walked on Our Hands,
Beatrice Schenk de Regniers **93-94**

from Jamboree, *David McCord* **14**

from Knitted Things, *Karla Kuskin* **36**

Lengths of Time, *Phyllis McGinley* **71-72**
Little Snail, *Hilda Conkling* **54**
Little Turtle, The, *Vachel Lindsay* **55**
Lo, the Winter Is Past, *The Bible* **29**

Mice, *Rose Fyleman* **63**
Mother, A, *Issa* **88**
Mrs. Peck-Pigeon, *Eleanor Farjeon* **81**
My Cat, Mrs. Lick-a-Chin, *John Ciardi* **61**
My Favorite Word, *Lucia and James L. Hymes, Jr.* **75**
Mysterious Cat, The, *Vachel Lindsay* **60**

Necks, *Rowena Bennett* **56**
Nicholas Ned, *Laura E. Richards* **91**

Nonsense Alphabet, *Edward Lear* **102**
North Wind Doth Blow, The, *Unknown* **32-33**

Oh Did You Hear?, *Shelley Silverstein* **91**
Old Man and the Cow, *Edward Lear* **96**
Old Man of Peru, *Unknown* **97**
Old Wife and the Ghost, The, *James Reeves* **38-39**
On Our Way, *Eve Merriam* **67**
Our Tree, *Marchette Chute* **18**

Pachycephalosaurus, *Richard Armour* **64**
Paper I, *Carl Sandburg* **70**
Paper II, *Carl Sandburg* **70**
Pig Tale, A, *James Reeves* **101**
Poem, *Langston Hughes* **77**
Politeness, *A. A. Milne* **73**
from Popcorn Song, A, *Nancy Byrd Turner* **25**
Prayer of the Little Ducks, The,
Carmen Bernos de Gasztold (Rumer Godden, tr.) **50**
Pumpkin, The, *Robert Graves* **37**

Rain, *Myra Cohn Livingston* **23**
Rain, *Robert Louis Stevenson* **23**
Rain Poem, *Elizabeth Coatsworth* **24**
Rain, Rain, Go Away, *Unknown* **21**
Rocks, *Florence Parry Heide* **89**

Snail, *John Drinkwater* **54**
Snow, *Issa* **87**
Snow Melting, *Ruth Krauss* **88**
So Long As There's Weather, *Tamara Kitt* **19-20**
Someone, *Walter de la Mare* **36-37**
Steam Shovel, The, *Rowena Bennett* **65**
Stopping by Woods on a Snowy Evening, *Robert Frost* **41**
Swing, The, *Robert Louis Stevenson* **84**

Tails, *Rowena Bennett* **56**
The More It Snows, *A. A. Milne* **26**
To a Red Kite, *Lilian Moore* **34**

To a Squirrel at Kyle-Na-No, *William Butler Yeats* **52**
To Meet Mr. Lincoln, *Eve Merriam* **76**

W, *James Reeves* **14**
We Must Be Polite, *Carl Sandburg* **73-74**
Weather, *Marchette Chute* **33**
Weather, *Eve Merriam* **22**
What in the World?, *Eve Merriam* **47-48**
What Is Pink?, *Christina G. Rossetti* **83**
What They Said, German Nursery Rhyme
(Rose Fyleman, tr.) **15-16**
When You Talk to a Monkey, *Rowena Bennett* **57**
Who Has Seen the Wind?, *Christina G. Rossetti* **30**
who knows if the moon's, *e. e. cummings* **85**
Who Lived in a Shoe?, *Beatrix Potter* **62**
Wind Song, *Lilian Moore* **31**
Windy Nights, *Robert Louis Stevenson* **30**
Winter Moon, *Langston Hughes* **82**
from Witch of Willowby Wood, The, *Rowena Bennett* **37**

Young Farmer of Leeds, A, *Unknown* **97**
Young Lady from Glitch, A, *Tamara Kitt* **96**

Subject Index

ABC's, 102
Animals
  ants, 67-68
  bats, 40
  bears, 28, 43-44, 56
  birds, 29, 32-33, 49, 53, 57-58, 81
  buffaloes, 52
  butterflies, 51
  camels, 56
  caterpillars, 51, 67-68
  cats, 47-48, 57-58, 60, 61
  cows, 96
  dinosaurs, 64, 65
  dogs, 49, 57-58, 59
  dormice, 32-33
  dromedaries, 56
  ducks, 48, 49, 50
  fireflies, 51, 87
  foxes, 44-45
  frogs, 47-48, 67-68
  giraffes, 56
  horses, 41, 88
  kangaroos, 56
  ladybugs, 15
  mice, 24, 47-48, 49, 62, 63
  monkeys, 47-48, 56, 57
  necks, 56
  Pachycephalosaurus, 64
  rabbits, 47-48
  snails, 54
  squirrels, 52, 100
  swans, 56
  tails, 56
  turtles, 55
  walking like, 67
Ants, 67-68
April Fool's Day, 91
Arithmetic, 99, 100, 101
Autumn, 18, 19

Bats, 40
Bears, 28, 43-44, 56
Birds, 29, 32-33, 49, 53, 57-58, 81
Buffaloes, 52
Butterflies, 51

Camels, 56
Caterpillars, 51, 67-68
Cats, 47-48, 57-58, 60, 61
Children, 47-48, 62, 67-68, 69, 84
Choral reading, 15-16, 25, 49, 60, 93-94, 100, 101
Christmas, 71
City settings, 21, 31, 65, 78-79, 81, 89
Clothes, 27, 28, 89

Clouds, 32
Colors, 83
Conservation, 52
Construction, 65
Cows, 96

Dinosaurs, 64, 65
Dogs, 49, 57-58, 59
Dormice, 32-33
Dromedaries, 56
Ducks, 48, 49, 50

Earth science
  hills, 84
  rocks, 89

Fall, 18, 19
Family, 69, 88, 93-94
Fireflies, 51, 87
Food, 14, 25, 91
Foxes, 44-45,
Friendship, 52, 77, 89
Frogs, 47-48, 67-68

Games, 25, 55, 67
Ghosts, 36-37, 38-39, 96
Giants, 43-44
Giraffes, 56

Halloween, 36, 37, 38-39, 43, 96
Hibernation, 28, 32-33
Hills, 84
Holidays and festivities, 72
  April Fool's Day, 91
  Christmas, 71
  Halloween, 36, 37, 38-39, 43, 96
  Lincoln's birthday, 76, 96
Horses, 41, 88
Houses, 78-79

Insects
  ants, 67-68
  caterpillars, 51, 67-68
  fireflies, 51, 87
  ladybugs, 15

Kangaroos, 56
Kites, 34

Ladybugs, 15
Limericks, 96, 97
Lincoln, 76, 96

Machines, 65
Manners, 49, 73-74
Metamorphosis, 51
Mice, 24, 47-48, 49, 62, 63
Monkeys, 47-48, 56, 57
Moon, 82, 85
Motherhood, 88
Music, 72
Mystery, 30, 36, 37. 38-39, 40, 41

Nonsense, 91, 92, 93-94, 94-95, 96, 97, 102
Nursery rhymes, 15-16, 21, 62, 102

Pachycephalosaurus, 64
Paper, 70
Popcorn, 25

Rabbits, 47-48
Rain, 19-20, 21, 22, 23, 24, 54, 89

Riddle-poems, 14, 32, 47-48
Rocks, 89
Rhyming fun, 14, 15-16, 19, 22, 27, 47-48, 92, 102
Rhythm activities, 25, 55, 67

Sad moods, 32, 52, 53, 77, 88
Sandwiches, 91
Seasons, 18, 19-20, 22
  autumn, 18, 19
  spring, 18, 19, 21, 22, 27, 29, 88
  summer, 18, 19, 22, 23, 54
  winter, 18, 19, 22, 23, 24, 25, 26, 27, 28, 29, 32-33, 41, 82, 87
Shadows, 82
Size, 67-68
Snails, 54
Snow, 25, 26, 41, 87, 88
Social studies
  conservation, 52
  construction, 65
  family, 69, 88, 93-94
  houses, 78-79
Songs, 25, 26, 29, 55
Spring, 18, 19, 21, 22, 27, 29, 88
Squirrels, 52, 100
Steam shovels, 65
Story poems, 38-39, 43-44, 44-45
Summer, 18, 19, 22, 23, 54
Swans, 56
Swinging, 84

Time, 71-72, 82
Toys, 57-58
Trees, 18
Turtles, 55

Walking, 67
Weather, 19-20, 87
  clouds, 32
  rain, 19-20, 21, 22, 23, 24, 54, 89
  snow, 25, 26, 41, 87, 88
  wind, 30, 31, 32, 33, 34, 54
Wind, 30, 31, 32, 33, 34, 54
Winter, 18, 19, 22, 23, 24, 25, 26, 27, 28, 29, 32-33, 41, 82, 87
Witches, 36, 37, 43-44, 96
Woods, 41
Words, 14, 15, 27, 75, 92